ANTONYMS

ANTHONY BARNETT

ANTONYMS

Anew

Barbs & Loves

A·B

*The reworked frontispiece image which first appeared on the cover
& title page of* Antonyms & Others, *2012, shows the shadow
of a leaf cutter ant carrying a leaf ~ & a bee*

First published 2016 by
ALLARDYCE BOOK ABP
14 Mount Street · Lewes · East Sussex BN7 1HL UK
www.abar.net

Distributed in USA by SPD
1341 Seventh Street · Berkeley CA 94710-1409
www.spdbooks.org

Typeset in Centaur MT with a leaf of
The Doves Type and Doves Type Pro
with first epigraph in Song
by AB©omposer
Proofs Tim Holmes
Printed by CPI ARowe EUK

CIP records for this book are available from
The British Library and The Library of Congress

ISBN 978-0-907954-53-8

NOTE

Antonyms I–VI appeared in the journal
of the English Association *The Use of English*
reprinted with revisions in
Antonyms & Others, Allardyce Book, 2012

Antonym VII appeared in *Antonyms & Others*

Antonyms VIII–XIV, XVI–XXI, XXIII, XXXI appeared in *Tears in the Fence*

Antonyms XV, XIX, XXVII appeared in *Snow lit rev*

Antonyms XXII, XXIV–XXVI, XXVIII–XXX, XXXII–XXXVIII
have not appeared anywhere else

There are some revisions here to earlier appearances

An earlier version of the poem in XXV "Leopardi and The Infinite"
was printed with a very short note as a separate insert enclosed with
InExperience and UnCommon Sense in Translation, Allardyce Book ABP, 2014

A mini version of just the opening of Antonym XXXI was posted online
at *Tears in the Fence* blog under the title "A Quick Note on César Vallejo"

The pieces appear here mostly in the order in which they were written
which is not in every case the order in which they first appeared

There are small variations in the style of bibliographic citations
dictated by what seemed appropriate when the pieces were written

My grateful thanks Ian Brinton and David Caddy

正言若反

一

gold begets black

ON A TRANSLATION

IT IS SO DISAPPOINTING when a rare opportunity is lost. I speak of *The Selected Poetry and Prose of Andrea Zanzotto* (University of Chicago Press, 2007)—though magnificent when, rarely, one is grasped, for example, Timothy Billings and Christopher Bush's two-volume Victor Segalen *Stèles* (Wesleyan University Press, 2007).

Ten years ago, in "Between the Recent Past and the Distant Present", Zanzotto, arguing his case, which does not immediately concern me here, commended the award of the Nobel Prize for Literature to his country-man Dario Fo. That was generous coming from the one poet who long may have deserved the prize before any other, presupposing socio-ethical acceptance of such ranking and prizing.

The trouble with editor-translator Patrick Barron's *Selected Zanzotto* is that it is a hodgepodge (or hotchpotch in Brit. usage) of new translations mixed up with previously published translations, without, as far as I can see, required revision, from a variety of sources, some good but others, such as *Selected Poetry of Andrea Zanzotto* (Princeton University Press, 1975), notably incompetent. Ruth Feldman and Brian Swann's versions therein suffered fourfold guilt: error (example: "German machine-guns" instead of "machine-guns Germans"); clumsiness through reductionist, explana-tory, normalized translations (example of the first: "cold jokes" instead of "stone cold jokes" for "barzellette freddissime"; example of the second: "ill-hatched from a cocoon" instead of "badly ecloded" for "male sbozzola-to", which Barron thinks fitting enough to keep for his own new version [why is perfect, perfectly formed, perfectly current, "eclode" not to be found in the current edition of the *OED*?]; example of the third: "—The woman teacher says so / Lewis and Alice say so." instead of "—Miss Teacher says so / Lewis and Alice says so." for "—La maestra lo dice / lo dice Lewis e Alice."); lack of imagination, or poetry (example, about the silkworm: "they go to the woods they moult / they rot they sleep like logs" instead of, for example, "they go to the shed go to shed / go to the dogs sleep like the dead" for "vanno al bosco vanno in muda / vanno in vacca dormono della quarta"). And the fourth? Failure to translate at all. Two examples: "The Elegy in Petèl". Why not "Elegy in Googoo"? (Beverly Allen in *Andrea Zanzotto: The Language of Beauty's Apprentice* [University of California Press, 1988] has a pretty ineffectual stab in "The Baby-Talk Elegy"); and "e 'vé paidi tut" accompanied by the translators' note "Veneto dialect for 'I had assimilated digested and expelled everything'." What's wrong with "took it in spat it out the lot"? That's my dialect. Oh, yes, and what exactly is "mini" doing for "nano"? Then there is the unthought through: Barron's "Strange name, dandelion" for "taràssaco", one of several designations Zanzotto uses for the herb in the same poem, is not strange. There are so many common or local English names from which to choose to try to match Zanzotto's. "Cranky name, cankerwort" gets it.

As well as poetry, Zanzotto is the author of several collections of exemplary poetic and critical essays. A feature of the Chicago selection, welcomed because it is a first, is the inclusion of a number of these. But again, there is a caveat, this time probably to be laid at the door of publisher rather than editor: there are not enough of them and they are relegated to the back, as if an afterthought, in lip service to a body of beautiful writing deserving no less than its own dedicated volumes. There is, then, a good long way to go before the totality, or even a satisfactory portion, of the work of this commentator's Nobel candidate receives proper care and consideration from professional English-language interpreters.

NOTE

"On a Translation" first appeared as Antonym 1 in *The Use of English* in 2009, two years before Zanzotto's passing. It draws on an unpublished paper "Some Poems Encountered in Translating the Problems of Andrea Zanzotto and Other Anecdotes of Literary Translation" presented in The Dark Room at *The Cambridge Conference of Contemporary Poetry*, 13 April 1991. It would be remiss were I not to acknowledge that I too of course am guilty of infelicity (I am told I have missed some Dante references—though not what they are) but I grappled and in places I came out tops. In fairness, in her co-translation with John P. Welle, I believe Feldman did better with *Peasants Wake for Fellini's Casanova and Other Poems* (Urbana, University of Illinois Press, 1977)

The drawing *A–Z of Mountain Paths* was done for the cover of *Poems by Andrea Zanzotto* (Allardyce Book, 1993), repr. with revisions and further poems in Anthony Barnett, *Translations* (Allardyce Book ABP, 2012)

A–Z of Mountain Paths

THE SERIOUS WRITER

WERE A YOUNG WOULD-BE WRITER of serious intent to ask: from whom among authors of the last century may I first and most learn? my choice would be the Austrian essayist and novelist Robert Musil, no matter what the language, at least European, beyond even, of our author or our would-be.

When Musil (1880–1942) is read in English it is usually as the author of a turn-of-the-century novel of adolescent sadism surrounding a military academy, *The Confusions of Young Törless*—translations with mildly differing titles have been snowballing—critically prescient of what would become the era of nazism and fascism, and his unfinished magnum opus *The Man Without Qualities*, an encyclopedic, in the word of one of its translators Burton Pike, novel of society, an empire, in free-fall. From the mesmerised protagonists' points of view this takes place in slow motion. There is also a volume of immaculate novellas, reissued as *Five Women* (previously *Tonka and Other Stories*), and a play *The Enthusiasts*. But for reason of wanting to draw attention to what I believe to be Musil's less considered non-fictional writings, I describe him here as essayist and novelist, not the other way round.

Since the 1980s such other works have been available in English in *Posthumous Papers of a Living Author* (Hygiene, CO, Eridanos, 1987; repr. New York, Archipelago, 2006), which, as the title declares, is not posthumous, *Precision and Soul: Essays and Addresses* (University of Chicago Press, 1990) and *Diaries, 1891–1941* (New York, Basic Books, 1999), along with new, alternative versions of the two novels. *Selected Writings* (New York, Continuum, 1986) includes alternatives of a few of the shorter pieces. Thus there is no longer excuse for ignoring the near totality of this essential author.

Doubtless it is unfashionable today to write the word "soul" though taken as it can be it remains nothing but relevant. In a 1922 essay "Helpless Europe" Musil writes of "an abiding miscommunication between the intellect and the soul. We do not have too much intellect and too little soul, but too little intellect in matters of the soul." Yet he is able to preface this "Digressive Journey" with "The author is more modest and less obliging than the title of this piece might lead one to infer. Indeed, I am convinced not only that what I say is wrong, but that what will be said against it will be wrong as well." Turning to his 1934 lecture "The Serious Writer in Our Time": "And because I am speaking about the serious writer and about today the beginning is easy, because I can confidently claim that we don't know what either one is." The lecture unfolds to show that while "we" may not know, Musil most certainly does.

Musil's insights, appreciations, critiques, are passionate and cucumber cool, pedagogic by accident and default. He shakes down the ramifications of psychology and morality and ethics and mores (or whatever else one can be comfortable with in calling and differentiating the like) while he tempers his stories with scepticism and comedy. An eloquent and robust prose appears to be well served by translators—though great novels are supposed to be capable of withstanding most anything, the reader who is not to be taken in making any necessary adjustments along the way—so that: should our serious young would-be need to read Musil in English, language will be no stumbling block.

Acerbic commentaries on cultural artifacts and personages, such as the penpusher and the paintspreader and the poet and the painter, prefigure his countryman Thomas Bernhard but where Bernhard's art requires him to be clear as mud, Musil is just clear. Musil, then, though radical in his fictional technique—Italo Svevo also comes to mind—is not an overt linguistic innovator in, for example, the Joycean sense; nor does he necessarily have to be upheld as the model of his time, and he is certainly not to be imitated—no one should be—but rather as a master and mentor of the theory and practice of the art and science of writing and critiquing. If the presumption that he does not figure high on most reading lists is not an injustice to the reader I hope I have offered some small, if inadequate, reasons why it might be a good idea if he did. For a start, my own thinking and writing would be better off were I myself to listen more often to my own advice. No or at least few illusions.

Musil has a short story "A Man Without Character" which, in the translation by Peter Wortsman, ends: "It was clear to me, if I may say so, that he would have liked to be himself again; but something held him back."

Words in Black and White

ANYONE LOOKING TO SUPPORT AN ARGUMENT for the stupidity or futility of cinema might be forgiven for thinking it is to be found in three vignettes by Osip Mandelstam and Joseph Roth but that is not proven. True, they do not devote enthusiastic attention to the subject elsewhere, unlike some other significant literary essayists of the period, for example, their compatriots Isaac Babel, who wrote screenplays based on his own and others' stories, and Robert Musil, who critically embraced the medium. Nevertheless, there is something to say about an uneasy relationship between literature and film, such as the way film can freeze, freeze frame, the viewer's imagination in a way that the reader's may not be. Nor do I think the examples I have chosen from the earlier days of the cinema are any the less valid for that.

In "I Write a Scenario" (circa late 1920s, unpublished in his lifetime), Mandelstam does pay ambiguous homage to a Russian master: "A magnificent frame in the style of Eisenstein immediately comes to mind [. . .]" Ambiguous because I do detect a note of irony. I also detect such a note in Roth's "The Cinema in the Arena" (*Frankfurter Zeitung*, 1925), his report of a screening in the open air, "no longer a church but a cinema", at Nîmes of *The Ten Commandments* "that great American film that has already been shown in Germany." "At a time when these commandments are not much obeyed," Roth writes, "that's already saying something."

To his quick chagrin, Mandelstam has been advised by an influential well-wisher, Shklovsky, who then does a disappearing act, leaving Mandelstam to his own devices, to write for the cinema: "I decided to try to write a scenario about the life of a fire brigade." "Then", "On the other hand", "Yes", "But, why", "What", "No", "Or maybe", "No, that's no good", "How about", "But", "All right". These are just some of Mandelstam's fits and starts to what he cannot finish. You have to read this hilarious piece in its brief entirety but until you have, unless you already have, Mandelstam finishes: "Film is not literature. One must think in frames. / Let the Fire Chief be on duty in the theater, while his friend treats his wife to pastries. / No, this is absurd. / My theme burned up in the creative process. My mind is blank. I've got to catch that Shklovsky."

Roth experiences a similar epiphany: "It was a good idea to put on a film in the old Roman arena. In such a cinema you come to comforting conclusions, as long as you look at the sky, rather than the screen." A few months later, in Marseilles, at the Cosmos, "A Cinema in the Harbour" (also *Frankfurter Zeitung*, 1925), there are ruckuses during the screening of a film entitled *Red Wolves*, among the children and among the adults too, among the latter because they do not approve of the tune being banged out on the accompanying piano. A father, after reassuring himself of his little ones' safety—they are seated either side of Roth—"turns to attend to whatever events are now in progress, be they on the screen or in some other part of the cinema." And Roth would like to turn the tables on the actors and the audience: "I like to imagine the robbers in the Abruzzi going to the cinema to see a film about the sea dogs of Marseilles." Roth has held on to his imagination.

There is, in fact, a most beautiful movie of Roth's prescient last, 1939, novella: *The Legend of the Holy Drinker* (1988). I remember it as beautiful, and I remember Roth's story, but I can hardly remember the film, because, I assume because, it is in colour—or is a small part of it in black and white? I would have to see it again.

Black and white movies are often those that I remember best, that I want to but do not have to see again. Two miraculous literary adaptations spring to mind. *Hunger* (1968) from the influential novel by Knut Hamsun. I do not think there has ever been a film more faithful to its turn-of-the-century original in its transfer to its new medium. *Mr Thank You* (1936) a gem of a full length feature cut—developed, I should say—from the tiniest of early tales by Kawabata about a chauffeur who thanks everyone he passes for making way for his bus on the narrow coastal roads between the provinces and the city. It is astounding how the passengers' lives are, yes, brought to life. I don't want to talk more about these films. I would just like you to see these examples of the unfrozen imagination—words in black and white—unless you already have.

NOTE

STORIES AND ESSAYS

Osip Mandelstam's "I Write a Scenario" is included in *The Complete Critical Prose and Letters*, trans. Harris (Ann Arbor, Ardis, 1979). Joseph Roth's "The Cinema in the Arena" and "A Cinema in the Harbor" are included in *Report from a Parisian Paradise: Essays from France, 1925–1939*, trans. Hofmann (New York, Norton, 2004), also as *The White Cities* (London, Granta,). Isaac Babel's screenplays are included in *The Complete Works*, trans. Constantine (New York, Norton, 2002). Robert Musil's "Cinema or Theater", for example, is included in *Precision and Soul: Essays and Addresses*, trans. Pike and Luft (University of Chicago Press, 1990). Yet in his lecture "On Stupidity", ibid., Musil could still jibe: "or it might perchance be the vacuously general, like the transformation of critical judgment by business, since God, in that goodness of his that is so hard for us to understand, has also bestowed the language of mankind on the creators of sound movies." Roth's *The Legend of the Holy Drinker*, trans. Hofmann (London, Chatto & Windus, 1989). Translations of Knut Hamsun's *Hunger* are Egerton (London, Duckworth, 1921), Bly (London, Duckworth, 1974), Lyngstad (Edinburgh, Cannongate, 1996). They are all good in their ways but I would like to suggest my own alternative to their opening sentences: "It was during the time I wandered about and starved in Kristiania, that passing strange city no one leaves before it has marked him." Kawabata Yasunari's "Thank You" (1925) is included in *Palm-of-the-Hand Stories*, trans. Dunlop and Holman (New York, Farrar, Straus and Giroux, 1988). There are later editions of all these.

FILMS

In Nîmes Roth sees *The Ten Commandments* directed by Cecil B. DeMille (1923) and in Marseilles *Red Wolves*, an unidentified, seemingly Italian, movie. *The Legend of the Holy Drinker* is an Italian film with an international cast, directed by Ermanno Olmi (1988). *Hunger* is a Nordic co-production, directed by Henning Carlson (1968). *Mr Thank You* is directed by Shimizu Hiroshi, who also wrote the screenplay (1936). The Japanese DVD *Arigatō-san* includes English subtitles.

The Notebook of José Saramago

José Saramago is a wonderful, in more senses than one, Portuguese novelist who won the Nobel Prize for Literature in 1998. I say is but I should say was because he died in June 2010 just two months after *The Notebook* appeared in English and two months short of a year following its last entry. But I prefer to say is because I am reading a notebook, *The Notebook*, as relevant in the present and, I think, the future, as it is in the recent past. *The Notebook* collects a year's blog entries posted by Saramago between September 2008 and August 2009, the almost daily task proposed by his wife Pilar and administrated with the assistance of two colleagues.

Now might be a good time to explain how the column in front of you came about. I reviewed a book for *The Use of English*. A bit of a mistake because our editor proposed I write more reviews. No, I did not want to. More than half in jest I suggested I contribute a series of "Antonym" commentaries. I had long harboured thoughts of such a weekly or monthly press column in which I might write about anything—rather in the manner of, for example, Montale, although it was posthumously revealed that such a regularity was too much so that many of the pieces under his byline were ghosted. Well, there has never been much of a tradition of the like being offered a serious poet here so that was not going to happen. Imagine my surprise when our editor jumped and said yes. My weekly or monthly is down to termly but never mind, I shall not need a ghost.

Why haven't I settled for a blog? I don't know. I only know that I resist it. Perhaps I simply do not like the word. I can think only of a bog blah blah. I have a lot to say though I do not always know how to say it and if I appear, only appear, impertinent enough to compare my little writings to Saramago's it becomes clear that I hardly know how to bring myself to say very much. It is then with admiration, and inspiration, that I read these celebrations and castigations of matters close to home and worldly by an extraordinary novelist. Saramago's subjects take in literary and non-literary friendships, Bush, Obama, Berlusconi, social and political and financial hope and injustice and corruption, the real and the ridiculous—things British get a couple of glancing blows—and, what especially concerns me for the moment, the Palestinian and Israel, to which he returns time and again. It puts me to shame that I omitted two poems in particular from my 2005 selected *Miscanthus* that were included in my 1987 collected *The Résting Bḛll*, and again in my 2012 collected *Poems &*.

Do
People change—
Or Israel
what can I do
or refuse you
as easily as I do
my birth.

✳

Here
O Israel
you are doing it here.
For all
pass over your rights
for all pass over
your safe conducts.
There is no doubt
you are quite
human
and henceforth
like anyone
else.

An entry in *The Notebook* "On the Impossibility of Such a Portrait", in which Saramago revisits a foreword he wrote to an exhibition catalogue of portraits of the multi-faceted poet reminds me that Pessoa *has another portrait* and therefore another heteronym of which I don't think he himself ever dreamt. In July 2008, two months before Saramago began his blog, I met up in Portugal with Prof. T from Tokyo who was there to deliver a paper on Irish literature. Strolling past a souvenir shop one of her delegate colleagues—from the Netherlands, if I remember correctly—spoke up: Look, they are selling mugs with a picture of James Joyce. Knowing that Durban, where Pessoa spent many early years, is not Dublin, it fell upon me, ungraciously perhaps, to disabuse the group of the idea that the whole of Oporto was celebrating the presence of an academic conference. No, I said, that's a likeness of the great Portuguese poet Fernando Pessoa. Was I mistaken? A few days later—no, it was earlier—T and I had visited Lisbon where we sat conversing with an exceptionally bronzed Pessoa at a table set before a favourite café A Brasileira. It didn't occur to me then to ask him.

Allow me a last conceit about Saramago. As I write I have in front of me a little letter signed José Saramago, Lanzarote, May 10, 2000. I had sent him, in the care of his publisher, my little book with a story "On the 31st July" in which the British Isles improves itself by irreversibly standing on its head during the course of a solar eclipse—it must have happened, at least I wish it had happened, because there is a satellite photo on the back of the cover to prove it. The narrator refers to two precedent geographical irregularities, one of them Saramago's *The Stone Raft* in which the Iberian peninsular breaks off from the Rest of Europe, in this event not without certain catastrophic consequences though restorative in the end. I feel honoured to have received the courtesy of Saramago's thank you—from an island in the Atlantic.

I had thought too to write about Saramago's delightful memoir *Small Memories* but I am already over my word limit. That may be reason enough to begin a blog baa baa but an explanation for my wariness has just occurred to me. In the wrong hands, with no editor or other moderating influence to say Enough, the web's potential for democracy easily turns to dictatorship, even if only of one.

NOTE

José Saramago, *The Notebook*, trans. Amanda Hopkinson and Daniel Hahn (London & New York, Verso, 2010). The two "Israel" poems were first printed in Anthony Barnett, *North North, I Said, No, Wait a Minute, South, Oh, I Don't Know (148 Political Poems)* (Lewes, privately printed, 1985), reprinted in *The Resting Bell* (Lewes, Allardyce, Barnett, 1987), and in *Poems &* (Lewes, Tears in the Fence, in assoc. Allardyce Book, 2012); the book that does not reprint them is *Miscanthus: Selected and New Poems* (Exeter, Shearsman, 2005). "On the 31st of July" is included in *Lisa Lisa: Two Prosays* (Lewes, Allardyce Book, 2000), and in *Poems &*, the precedent geographical irregularities being Cees Nooteboom's *In the Dutch Mountains* (English trans. 1987), in which the Pyrenees take themselves off to the Netherlands, or vice versa, and Saramago's *The Stone Raft* (English trans. 1994). There is a curious editorial error in the first, hardback, edition of the translation of *The Notebook* in footnoting the origin of Saramago's Pessoa foreword to the catalogue *Fernando Pessoa: A Galaxy of Poets, 1888–1935*, the title of a library and theatre foyer small exhibit presented by the London Borough of Camden in assoc. with the Portuguese Ministries of Foreign Affairs and Culture in October 1985, with a rather pedestrian foreword by José Blanco, chair of the exhibition committee. Saramago's imaginative foreword appeared in the catalogue to a different, substantial, exhibition, *Um Rosto para Fernando Pessoa: obras de trinta e cinco artistas portugueses contemporâneos* (Lisboa, Centro de Arte Moderna da Fundação Calouste Gulbenkian, 1985), which is referenced in the former. And, no, much as one might wish to entertain the idea José Blanco is not a pen name for Saramago. In consequence of my communication to the translators the error is corrected in the subsequent paperback printing. Saramago's *Small Memories* (English trans., 2009) encapsulates a childhood.

The review referred to in paragraph two considered some books about George Oppen. It appeared in *The Use of English*, vol. 60, no. 2 (spring 2009)—see now Antonym xxxii fol.

AI WEIWEI'S BLOG

Just when *Antonyms & Others* (2012) is ready for press a selection from a remarkable more-than-daily blog of equally human proportions from the other side of the world, tempered with what on this side of the world are impassioned and deadpan ironies, also makes it to print: *Ai Weiwei's Blog: Writings, Interviews, and Digital Rants, 2006–2009*, ed. & trans. Lee Ambrozy, & others (Cambridge, MA, & London, WritingArt Series, MIT Press, 2011): "The whole city is like a poorly assembled and cheap stage where all the people passing through it—men, women, the young, and the old—were nothing more than props, all part of an unsightly performance on culture, history, and political achievements."—from the entry "Different Worlds, Different Dreams", trans. Eric Abrahamsen. "It is the same under any dynasty: there are too many people here with ordinary trifles, sharing their pains and joys. One thing remains constant: these pains and joys are all fragmentary, they cannot be truly described or expressed, they cannot be multiplied or rendered, they can only be sensed, they are unutterable."—from the entry "Hypnosis and Fragmented Reality: Li Songsong", trans. Philip Tinari. In fact, there are many pages from which one might wish to quote. On the damage done to Tibet: "I will never visit that place, even if there were increasingly modern means of transportation. There is no reason, and no need to go. I want to learn how to maintain the distance between us."—from the entry "A Road with No End". Originally, Ai was invited, obliged almost, to blog by the authorities, those same authorities who closed him down in 2009. The blog is well read alongside *Ai Weiwei Speaks*, with Hans Ulrich Obrist (London, Penguin, 2011). A confession: I visited Ai's 100 million hand-painted ceramic sunflower seeds in the Turbine Hall at Tate Modern in 2010. I stole a handful, two handfuls in fact, in sight of a notice saying don't. My justification was an interview in which Ai said that if he were a visitor he would take one (he did not say a handful, or two handfuls, it is true) but I would have done it anyway. I began to give them away at Christmas in little boxes with a note that reads do not eat forever keep.

The Artist ['muŋk] Tries to Speak

Publication of a magnificent six-volume illustrated edition of *Vincent van Gogh: The Letters* (London, Thames & Hudson, 2009), brilliantly annotated and contextualized, reminds that the writings of another painter, also translated into English, have not fared so well.

The Story of Edvard Munch (London, Arcadia, 2001) by Norwegian novelist and romantic pianist Ketil Bjørnstad, the original published in 1993, fictionalizes in 386 monstrous pages the artist's life through an injudicious extracting from the letters and notebooks, his own and his contemporaries', interspersed with recast press reports and the author's clod-hopping present-tense interference. In Torbjørn Støverud and Hal Sutcliffe it has better translators than it deserves. The supposed reality (I suppose) of the narrating does nothing to dispel the myths, which are in dire need of being dispelled. Why, why, why, cannot Munch be left to speak for himself? All that is needed, all that is wanted, is the mass of Munch's own writings. Annotated, yes. Messed with, no.

Very few artists have left such a legacy of literacy so it is better to settle for Poul Erik Tøjner's *Munch: In His Own Words* (Munich, Berlin, London, New York, Prestel, English ed., 2003 [the original 2001, it would appear]). At least this delightfully presented largish format book places the selections from Munch's writings in sensible and relevant contexts, among photos and colour reproductions. Tøjner's at times overstressed, at times naïve, commentary is easily forgiven because of his perceptions: "There is one constant element that is more significant than all others in Munch's work and that is the glance—the eye. If one wants to see people looking, one need go no further than the work of Munch. Few other painters have painted the eye, painted sight, painted the glance, painted the gaze, or the look, to the same degree." The facing page reproduction of *Portrait of the Artist's Sister Inger* illustrates, in its full-frontal intensity, one aspect of Tøjner's observation.

So, it was with eager anticipation that, while preparing this piece, I chanced upon what I did not know: *The Private Journals of Edvard Munch: We Are Flames Which Pour Out of the Earth* (Madison, University of Wisconsin Press, 2005). Here, surely, I would find a substantial presentation of Munch's writings, even if doubtless again just a selection of them, left to speak for themselves. I needn't have bothered and, I suppose (that suppose again), I might have been forewarned by the choice of an only seemingly appropriate quotation for the subtitle. The book is a scrappy editing job—and this despite the, as so often, fulsome grant and other assistance acknowledgements—though, I have no reason to doubt, otherwise more or less adequately translated. "Left to speak for themselves", I wrote a moment ago. I should say so, though not quite in the way I was envisioning.

"I have not tried to follow any chronological order in organizing the sections", editor and translator J. Gill Holland writes. But there are no delineated sections unless a few black and white plates of lithographs and drypoints somewhere over halfway through are supposed to divide things in two. I don't think so. What the editor presents are sequentially numbered texts, all of which look like poems. Except that many of them are nothing to do with poems or any other kind of imaginative writing but are, for example, concerned with the everyday, and the numbering bears no relation to anything in Munch or the Munch archive. There is no context, no annotation, only a generalized discursive introduction. The reader new to these, by turns reasoned and impassioned, writings will find no indication whether the poem-look is Munch's—deliberate or simply tracking the shape of the space available on the page on which he wrote—or the editor's interpretation or intervention. The game is given away by Frank Høifødt's perfunctory foreword: "A complete and scholarly presentation belongs to the future." Why? Why the future? Why not now? Why not before now?

It is to Tøjner's work, not referenced by Holland, that one must turn for answers and insights through reproductions of some of the manuscripts, often in variously coloured paints and crayons and childlike caps. The typography, here in Jennifer Lloyd's translation, mostly respects the uppercase of the painterly poems and imaginings as opposed to the more normal writing of the prosaic journal entries, quotidian, verging on the philosophical, contemplating painting and loving and journeys abroad. There are inconsistencies in this presentation but where there are I can see why and doubtless they were a designer's choice.

Valuable literature of one sort or another is to be found among only a handful of painters close to our times. Van Gogh for one. Munch for another. The new edition, however welcomed, of van Gogh's writings is the latest of several. But of Munch's, until that long overdue "complete and scholarly presentation", or simply a trustworthy reading edition, materializes, we continue to have, both in the original and in translation, only a glimpse and if one picks up the wrong book a befuddled one at that.

THE TREE OF KNOWLEDGE

FOR

BETTER OR FOR WORSE

NOTE

It is pleasing to report that the Munch Museum in Oslo has begun to publish English, French and German translations of Munch's writings at least online at www.emunch.no

LETTER TO A PHOTOGRAPHER

"Jack isn't making himself clear. If these duties were not imposed on us by the masters, it's obvious that we should not strive to perform them well in the masters' presence and badly in their absence. We should just perform them!" is a passage from Louis-René des Forêts's story "The Children's Room", in which an apparent auditory voyeur, ear to the door—an eavesdropper though voyeur seems a much more appropriate word—listens to a group of children quasi-philosophically discussing and acting out a scenario of idiotic school rules. He says apparent because by the end of the story, at the end, the overhearer is revealed not to be the immoralist the reader has been led to believe. He will not give the game away.

For many months he has been engaged in translating Louis-René des Forêts's *Poèmes de Samuel Wood*, a meditation on life and language and loss, the loss of others who are loved as well as of the self. And now this task he has set himself, for whatever unclear reason, unless it is clear, is almost done.

In the hope of gaining some last minute insight into the work, which might improve though not perfect his translation, he has turned to reading some other works by des Forêts. (He pauses here to reflect on a group of excitedly chattering children in uniform, composed mainly but not entirely of girls, just passing the café window table at which he is sitting writing. Oh, here comes another. There goes another.) Among them a volume he has owned for many years that collects a novel and some stories but that he had thought he had neglected by giving it only an occasional cursory glance, always to give up on it. But this is not true. As he begins to read he realizes he has already read it through and through. For example, the story "The Great Moments of a Singer" is set in London. He recognizes the dark cloud that descends upon him as the word appears on the page. A cloud that descended when last he read it because of the reality, or the bad dream, of that city in which he believes himself terribly hurt by the past. And there in the story "Disorderly Silence", set among the tyranny of pupils and teachers, which perhaps has the salutary effect of giving him to understand that he has never really been alone in such experiences, is the visible mark of his previous reading, his writing in the margin wondering about the translation of a particular word. (It doesn't matter which.)

Dear Sh, he writes (which may be her name or shy or hush): I know that you have told me that it is time to stop writing and to draw.

Can it be that she who knows beautifully how to take a photograph and make a drawing (though he has yet to see more than one such drawing in a little notebook) beyond and before the taking and the making of mere gestures, though she says it is difficult, can possibly hold in esteem his little things, which is all he can call them? Or is he being teased? Or is he being bashful? Or neither or both? But he knows it cannot be true that he is an artist because writing comes to him only with difficulty, whereas these little squiggles of his come easily, so long as he always sticks to the first attempt. If he tries to redo them they never work. So he is a writer. He has to write. He has to do what is difficult. Even if he cannot write at all. And here is a conundrum, a double bind: if he does not write, when he cannot write, because he is lazy, which sometimes he certainly is, or because of some more substantial cause, his predisposition to anxiety increases. Yet, when he is writing, when he can write, he is wracked with guilt, unless wracked be too strong a word, because that is not what was supposed to be in store for him, though the very early insistence of others that he should read and read must have given him a head start. A regret?

How impatient he is to finish this now, he who pretends (does he really pretend?) to believe an old saw (he has repeated it so often) of intellectual strength and emotional vulnerability. He refuses the more honest word weakness. Quite the coward.

He has made a drawing to accompany his translation of Louis-René des Forêts's *Poèmes de Samuel Wood*. It is supposed to be a tree. But looking at it now he sees that it is also an uncanny likeness of its author—or perhaps

Samuel Wood. He finds this extraordinary and mysterious. For a moment he allows himself to escape writing and to be the artist she would like him to be.

NOTE

The Children's Room (Calder, 1963), Jean Stewart's translation renders Jacques as Jim; here he is reinstated as Jack; *Poèmes de Samuel Wood* (Fata Morgana, 1988); *Poems of Samuel Wood* (Allardyce Book, 2011); repr. with corrections in Anthony Barnett, *Translations* (Tears in the Fence, in assoc. Allardyce Book ABP, 2012)

The Publisher

It was very kind of her to invite me to one of her salon evenings. I was very glad I said no, graciously at first, later intemperately. I have only myself to blame for unwittingly setting the whole thing up because I contacted her in the first place with a forthright comment, I couched it politely, about something to do with one of her good authors, though the comment was about something not so good, about an English *critic, anthologizer, memoirist*, in fact a *mediocrity*, whose misdemeanours included offences against myself and my erstwhile colleagues, with whom she had put her interesting German author in conversation, at one of her salon evenings. She responded with what I did think was suspiciously unjustified enthusiasm and generosity, I was momentarily taken in, because I wanted to be, I am now confirmed in interpreting first and foremost her desire to cultivate a literary contact who might turn out to be useful. Well, she didn't know me, did she, so she should have been more circumspect before deciding to think of someone such as myself as an opportunity. Somewhere in the back of my mind, if not further forward, I expect, though to be honest, I agree, I saw her like that too. Nevertheless, she did say she would like to see a poem or two, as if I could agree to make such a miniscule pick from what I wrote in clusters, racemes, chords, not to be pulled apart too severely, so to speak. How was she to understand why I would not attend her soiree at which one of *those* poets would be reading, or even if one of *these* poets were to be. How was she to know. Siren at the fountain. How could I possibly explain why to one so intent on entertaining the worst of that band of editors and scribblers, that circus of a cabal, though there is nothing much secret about it, going round and around rewarding each member in turn with a poison, a prize, a review, a publication. So I packaged up some books and took them to the post office. I thought at least some of the translations might be of interest to her, right up her metropolis street, I thought. You see, I am living in what seems to be a cross between The

Fairy Tale Town and The Little Town Where Time Stood Still. I haven't heard a thing. And I must remember not to make my writing too small, I keep telling myself, or lean too far out of a window for that matter.

A few hours after deciding this must be the finish a message arrived *I am impressed.* (But where to put the emphasis . . .) If I fail to add this I shall be doing her a disservice, leaving the impression she must indeed have taken umbrage, she was perfectly entitled to, though it does no justice to a satisfactory ending.

I haven't heard anything else, oh yes, press releases.

NOTE

"The Fairy Tale Town" is the title of a story by Robert Walser, who wrote in a microscript; *The Little Town Where Time Stood Still* is the title of a novel by Bohumil Hrabal, who leant too far out. Other literary references are anybody's guess—not anyone's, anybody's.

BLOOD ON THE THROAT

WHAT TO DO WITH THE POEM THAT OPENS "All those whose hearts are an inkblot in a child's copybook all those whose word is an embrace broken in a final effort of terrestrial gigantism"? Excise it, which is what Aimé Césaire did to "Torture" and almost half the other poems in his 1948 collection *Soleil cou coupé* when he recast it in 1961 for one of two sections of *Cadastre*. That's the version that appeared in Césaire's *The Collected Poetry*, translated by Clayton Eshleman and Annette Smith (University of California Press, 1983). Now, for the first time *Solar Throat Slashed: The Unexpurgated 1948 Edition* is published in a translation by A James Arnold—head editor of Césaire's complete works in French—with Clayton Eshleman (Wesleyan University Press, 2011).

Who can begin to know why Césaire ripped apart his poems, excising so many, altering others, leaving untouched just twelve of seventy-two. A & E offer explanations—Césaire had, incidentally, published two markedly different versions of *Cahier d'un retour au pays natal*, both 1947—but it is not my competence to go over that ground. Suffice to say that Césaire's practical and theoretical politics bore heavily on him and the collection became less seemingly surreal—though his André Breton-lauded images served a more rigorous purpose—to poetry's detriment. As Arnold writes: "Consequently, the modernist poetry Césaire had practiced throughout the 1940s, and which reached its full fruition in the 1948 edition of Soleil cou coupé, was substantially obliterated."

There is quite a distance between the Soleil of the title, found as the last line of Guillaume Apollinaire's "Zone" (*Alcools*, 1913), and the earthbound register of the 1961 redaction in *Cadastre*. Or is there? Another excised poem (A & E use eliminated, which I do not like) is "The Sun's Knife-Stab in the Back of the Surprised Cities". No distance at all then. Nor, by the way, do I like "Unexpurgated". Expurgated smacks of an external imposition.

Nevertheless, the translation is quite serviceable for a bilingual edition, treading a line between literality and inspiration. Occasionally I would want to tinker, with the title "Le coup de couteau du soleil dans le dos des villes surprises", for example. "The Sun's Knife-Stab" is not wrong but how much more force simply "The Sun's Stab" would have or even "The Sun's Stab with a Knife". And in "Several Miles from the Surface" why is "sur le coup de trois heures après midi" rendered "at the stroke of 3 p.m." and not "three in the afternoon" or "three o'clock"? That sort of thing. But that is to carp. I think Eshleman comes out better in his Césaire collaborations than he does in his versions of another great modernist, César Vallejo. Certainly, I find I have made fewer notations in the margins of his Césaires than I have his Vallejos.

✻

I had thought I had met D. S. Marriott through Andrew Crozier, his university mentor. But this morning out walking I remember it was another of Crozier's students who first introduced us. She had the nous. (Such a clever word but let's be clear, apropos a sonnet by Keston Sutherland, the best nous Adorno ever had was his moi.)

This is a moment to note that Allardyce, Barnett came close to bringing out Marriott's first full-length collection of poems. It was typeset but professional and personal issues conspired to stop its appearance. In truth, by the time Marriott thought he wanted this, ABP was no longer in a good position to take responsibility for the work of others. However, more years allowed what was scheduled in 2001 as "A Ship Called Lubek" to be substantially reordered and augmented as *Incognegro* (Salt, 2006), dedicated to Crozier.

That Marriott reads Césaire is to be expected and, indeed, is obvious. One poem is entitled "Notebook of a Return", also the title of the second of the two sections of *Incognegro*—while "La fierté de la chair" in the later *The Bloods* is dedicated in his memory—but it is hard to discern literary as opposed to historical political influence. A great deal of Marriott's pre-*Incognegro* work is characterized by an immense luxuriant vocabulary, in danger of swamping thinking and cadence in ways that Césaire's images do not. Suddenly Marriott learns to take control. Here is the first stanza of "At Chartres":

Below the fields and pathways
& fifty-five-gallon drums
              on fire with deep blue flame,
I find myself caught wide-eyed & dumb
in the masses,
              trying very hard to be 'public'
but the people are sweating & my mouth hangs—
the tins are too heavy
              & the fish are strapped to my back—
people crowd round the fires to warm themselves
as if this were Lord Hideyoshi's Castle,
    the tour of its splendour
                          a mirror to the whole world:
    forced to pass along the *engawa*
        as black thunder strides across the level earth.

I love this and the rest of this poem. I wonder at what Lord Hideyoshi, who rose to high position from the lowliest of beginnings, is doing here— actually, his Castle—until I learn that the laws he enacted had the virtual effect of abolishing the slavery endemic in his country. But, if it is not that, it doesn't matter. It is a poem I can trust.

Marriott often sings through historical others. John Wilkinson, who figures in one of the more plainly personal poems, points to this in a cover puff: "—history, place and others' recognitions." Sometimes this is to be trusted, other times not. Then I am stopped short unsure of the speaking voice. Wilkinson himself I have lately berated for descent into untrustworthiness of a different clever sort, specifically in certain critical writings. (Marriott's are constructively thoughtful.)

"Others' recognitions" carry over into Marriott's next two volumes in various cadences. Again, who is speaking? "Ishmael, Negro" begins "Today is Sunday. / Nothing disturbs, as expected," *Hoodoo, Voodoo* (Shearsman, 2008). And "The Dog Enchanter": "What if he were to set off / panting through the ruins / swishing his tail", *The Bloods* (Shearsman, 2011). But, Marriott distinguishes himself in undertaking a reconciliation of classical and modernist languages—Greece is never far from his Black beat: "We sent our letters back to Jerusalem / and got back to work." "Greeking", *The Bloods*. That it does not always jell only highlights the occasions when it does.

Marriott wrote his doctoral thesis on J. H. Prynne but his poetry is a far cry from Post-Prynnean Apostlyptic practice. The point is, Marriott transcends cleverness just as, for all their differences, Césaire—whose voice is always his—does. It is time for Marriott to be as great, as he can be.

What, then, to do with the poem that ends "O all those whose gaze is a carousel of birds born of a superhuman balance of sponges and of fragments from a galaxy extinguished beneath a little station's heel" but to restore it and forget the affected cleverness of this essay.

NOTE

A & E's translation of "le talon d'une petite gare" unnecessarily reads "a small railway station's heel", which, I think, impedes the line. Also, of course, it may be that it really should read "talon".

Love Letters

No one is seriously funnier than Bohumil Hrabal but what I want to talk about here is a writer's view of love expressed to his wife in the unpunctuated autobiographical novel *Vita Nuova*. I quote at length so that I shall not have to write very much myself: "Darling if you treat me nice I'll teach you to write too It's nothing you couldn't get a handle on look here every love-struck boy or girl writes love letters and those love letters are actually ad hominem communiqués and everyone who's written those reams of love-struck letters in a certain sense is already a poet because those romantic missives are filled with such a profusion of drivel that here and there some of that nonsense resembles beautiful literature I'll wager you wrote that Jirka of yours a novelful of letters admittedly not quite like Goethe's own *Sorrows of Young Werther* but you were in love and perhaps still are and those sorts of love-struck letters those love stories that end up tucked away somewhere tied in a little ribbon are the genesis of great writing so darling this is what ties all of us together even as kids we wrote little messages and stuffed them into chinks of the tombs at the cemetery and in summer we wedged those letters into the cracked earth because those letters were the real McCoy for our eyes only and that's the beginning of real writing . . . I write a sort of love-struck correspondence myself not to women or to the objects of my own romantic erotic desires anymore but I write letters addressed to the elements I send them out to the beautiful little animals and to the trees and to the buildings and to those pubs of mine like I was writing to a beautiful girl . . . I write like a hairdresser in love or like a mechanic in love or you take your pick because when people come across those letters years later they can't believe their eyes the beautiful images they created the beautiful emotions they were capable of expressing But a writer continues with those lovestruck letters he spends his whole life writing those love-struck messages to the world".

An opposite view appears to be held by Czesław Miłosz. Cynthia L. Haven tells this story in a 2011 *World Literature Today* article about Julia Hartwig: "She was dissuaded early from the well-trod staples of a young woman's poetry. During the war she visited Miłosz for the first time, traveling from Lublin to Miłosz's Warsaw home. She had brought a handful of her own poems, and those of a girlfriend. / His reaction might have dismayed a woman of weaker will. As she recounted it in a 2005 interview, he said, 'Oh, about love . . . Love is not a topic for poems.' But he did the poet a big favor, forcing her to dig deeper for less obvious material. / 'I don't think he really was enchanted, you know?' she drawled in her living room, and laughed."

Will an examination of Miłosz's poems bear this out? I open his *Collected* at random. On the left hand page I read "for I believed despair could last and love could last." ("Whiteness", Paris, 1966). On the right hand page: "—Love of God is love of self," ("Thesis and Counter-Thesis", Berkeley, 1962). Probably this does not tell very much. So, again, at random: "I was ready to tear out the heart of the earth with a knife" ("The Spirit of the Laws", Washington, D.C., 1947). Again: "Confess, you have hated your body, / Loving it with unrequited love. It has not fulfilled / Your high expectations." ("From the Rising of the Sun: VI. The Accuser", Berkeley, 1973–1974). Again? No, I give up. Certainly, there is cerebral passion and eroticism in Miłosz's poems but is there, what shall I say, true love, or the belief of true love? That being love-struck? His counsel to Hartwig might not be flummery but Haven has a caution: "I sense that Miłosz was simply dismissing a romantic teenage girl, rather than laying down any immutable laws about poetry."

Roger Giroux in *Blank* speaks with Hrabal, though in the more sedate, refined, voice of the vine as opposed to the hop: "A self-respecting 'writer' has the duty to write only love letters. All the rest is servility and scribbling." And "The membrane and the quivering flesh of the poem originate in the same initial cell, initially stimulated by the VERB-I-IS-LOVE." So to Miłosz a last random time: "A coelentera, all pulsating flesh, animal-flower, /

All fire, made up of falling bodies joined by the black pin of sex." ("With Trumpets and Zithers", Berkeley 1965).

And what of Julia Hartwig herself? Haven quotes from "Return to My Childhood Home": "Yet happy moments come to me from the past, like bridesmaids carrying oil lamps." I cannot say that Miłosz does not write love letters but the ones I would like to receive are written by others.

NOTE

Roger Giroux, *Blank: (The Invisible Poem)*, trans. Anthony Barnett (Allardyce Book, 2001); repr. with corrections in Anthony Barnett, *Translations* (Tears in the Fence, in assoc. Allardyce Book ABP, 2012)

Irena Grudzinska Gross, *Czesław Miłosz and Joseph Brodsky: Fellowship of Poets* (Yale University Press, 2009) cites the March 26, 2005 interview with Hartwig by Jarosław Mikołajewski in *Wysokie Obcasy*. Hartwig has also told her Miłosz anecdote to Haven and others

Julia Hartwig, *In Praise of the Unfinished: Selected Poems* (Knopf, 2008); *It Will Return: Poems* (Northwestern University Press, 2010) both trans. John and Bogdana Carpenter

Cynthia L. Haven, "Invisible You Reign Over the Visible: Julia Hartwig's Reality Mysticism", *World Literature Today*, vol. 85, no. 4 (University of Oklahoma, July–August 2011)

Cynthia Haven, email correspondence with AB (16 October 2011, 14 November 2011) which includes the caution, quoted with her kind permission

Bohumil Hrabal, *Vita Nuova: A Novel*, trans. Tony Liman (Northwestern University Press, 2010)

Czeslaw Milosz, *The Collected Poems, 1931–1987*, various trans. (Ecco Press, 1988; Viking/Penguin, 1988)

PATRIMONY OF AFFECTATION:
ON KNOWING INTRODUCTIONS

"IN THE TWENTY-FIRST CENTURY, everyone wants a piece of Mina Loy."
Probably rhetorical to wonder why Dr Crangle sullies her introduction to
an important research and recovery: *Stories and Essays of Mina Loy* (Dalkey
Archive, 2011) with that piece of gratuitous off-putting distraction. To
point to the obvious, quite who "everyone" is, I don't know. Might as
well say "everyone wants a piece of Veronica Forrest-Thomson" or—more
later. Probably Crangle does. It takes one to know one. She would know.

Don't—those who happen to know more than it is relevant to reveal
here—imagine that this is just my opportunity to take a personal swipe.
Of course it is that but it is also a very objective objection to frequently
encountered objectionables in certain editor or translator introductions
that go beyond a sober remit, that affect to know too much, that lack
probity in favour, I might say at risk myself of being taken to task, of the
proprietary. Doesn't Crangle herself take a large slice of Mina Loy whilst
pretending not to? Or rather, isn't she claiming, by barely concealed im-
plication, that she is the one with the proprietary right? While I'm at it, I
can't resist this gem: "The significance of handwritten dashes has become
something of a sore point in the study of Emily Dickinson's manuscripts
and poems, and I want to steer clear of unduly fetishising Loy's dashes here."

Done with Crangle, I turn to an arch villain in such matters. The estimable translator from German, Michael Hofmann.* I thank him for his
perseverance in seeing the translation and publication of essential works
by Joseph Roth, a truly great writer of the twentieth-century, to near com-
pletion—though Hofmann is not the only one. But what's this: "Briefly
atop this heap of literary coral, I feel a modicum of triumph, a degree of
shame, and a strong sense of being at a loss. 'Und dann? Und dann?' as my
father would sometimes say, 'What next? What next?' "—introduction to
Rebellion. Frankly, dear, I don't give a dann. Or this: "phrases to kill for"—

introduction to *Report from a Parisian Paradise* aka *The White Cities*. Some objectionables can be hard to pin down. It's often a matter of tone. Breezy familiarity, peppered adjectives of the "utterly", "tremendously" sort, utterly (oh dear) wrong-headed jarring allusions, Heaney, Jarrell. Until we reach Roth's *A Life in Letters*. Not hard to pin down now. If Hofmann's introduction and copious annotations weren't frequently so outrageous that they take on the aspect of a bad joke, it would be anger, not guffaws or a weary shake of the head, raising the hypertension. Actually, his opening salvo at those to whom Roth did not write does come close to inciting anger: "Nothing to parents (but Joseph Roth never saw his father, Nahum, who went mad before he knew he had a son, and reacted to his overproud and overprotective mother, Miriam, or Maria, to the extent that he sometimes claimed to have her pickled womb somewhere)" and so on. Apart from anything else, it's a bad sentence. It wouldn't be to flinch from interesting contextual information to wait a while for that. Annotations to individual letters, at random: "There is perhaps no better instance of Roth's superb and aggressive pure-mindedness (which was certainly the death of him as much as anything else) than this refusal to participate in such a venture, which so characterizes our 'postmodern' epoch."; "of course and still refers to *The Radetsky March.*"—what's with that "of course"?; "Really a bizarrely, almost provocative insouciant note to go from someone in Zweig's position to someone in Roth's." That'll do.

I am almost sorry to go to town on Hofmann. It could have been any number of others. I am not, for example, the slightest bit interested in reading Murakami Haruki's self-regarding life story, which he relates as an introduction to Natsume Sōseki's *Sanshirō* (Penguin, 2009). Where there has to be an introduction—they are often indulgences, from which translations of poetry may suffer more often than fiction—I look for a minimum of guidance, the barest helpful context, the righting of wrongs. I don't want to have to scribble scathing comments, make strike-through cancellations, rip out offending pages, not buy the book. I don't want my reading pre-empted. I have my own thinking to do.

Since Michael Hofmann did bring his dad into the equation, what about Gert Hofmann? *Lichtenberg and The Little Flower Girl* (CB Editions, 2008) is a charming little story. But what is a teddy bear doing in eighteenth century Germany? Is that Gert's or Michael's doing? Is that funny or not? Oh, I just threw that in.

Not quite done. Quite a disgraceful slice—monstrous slab more like it—of Grace Lake cake Crangle at University of Sussex seeks from the European Research Council, under the self-serving aggrandizing non-subject rubric Preserving and Promoting the Avant-Garde: from England to Europe (Short Name/Acronym): PAGE. Whether she gets it or not I know not. Better had the Lake–Mendelssohn papers gone to the new Poetry Archives in Cambridge University Library, a venture that was about to take off. If they belong anywhere in this mired—of course it cannot always be admirable—grove of academe they belong there. Whatever, it's cowpat. Tant pis.

* POSTSCRIPT

Estimable? I wonder. My Vienna colleague Konrad Nowakowski explains, for example, *just* for example, that in the opening paragraph of "His K. and K. Apostolic Majesty" in *The Hotel Years*, where Roth is meaningfully syntactically complex, Hofmann is simplistically colloquial and, I might add, colloquial or not, sloppily ungrammatical. Are we in for the affliction of the easier read? Not content with that, Hofmann is true to his aversion agenda in dropping Roth's dedication of that article *Für Stefan Zweig*. Hardly his job. When it comes to *The Radetzky March*, of which there are three earlier translations—quite why Penguin thought Joachim Neugroschel's a fit replacement, however much one may be desirable, for Eva Tucker's revision of Geoffrey Dunlop's original is a puzzle—I am assured that Hofmann's is incompetent. But, fortunately, one cannot snuff out all of the life in the work of a great writer so easily.

I SING THE BOOKMARK. No, silly, not those on the laptop. They're not really bookmarks. I don't think they should be called bookmarks. I don't know what they should be called. And I don't sing fancy metallic or fabric bookmarks. I might have sung parchment bookmarks in a past era. I sing the paper bookmark and the card bookmark. Or the leaf bookmark. A new leaf or a leaf in fall. Paper on paper. Leaf on leaf.

Not only is my page lost without my bookmark, I am lost. I am in bed reading. Suddenly I am panic stricken. My arms flail about. Almost involuntarily. Which is why I did not write I flail my arms about. I jump up. Frantic. I utter an expletive. Where is it? Where's my bookmark? Where has my bookmark gone? I can't go on reading until I find my bookmark. Is it on the bedside chest? Is it among the bed covers? Is it on the floor? I've succeeded in shutting my book. I didn't mean to. I've lost my page. I utter another expletive. I'm lost. This is hardly an exaggeration. O my bookmark. Here it is. Among the folds of the bed covers covering my chest. Right under my nose. What a fuss. I settle back on the pillow. Calm restored. I find my page. I carry on reading secure in the knowledge that now my bookmark is within easy reach on the bedside chest, placed there with a concentrated determination to remember exactly where it is.

Let's look at some of my favourite bookmarks. Favourites at the moment. This one is a postcard. A detail of *Pilgrims on the Slopes of Mount Fuji* by Zeshin. At the moment it is bookmarking *Modus Vivendi*, essays by Gunnar Ekelöf, a book that has stood on a particular shelf for quite a few years without, until now, my reading it from start to finish or, rather, middle to finish then start to middle—If the two couples jabbering away about prize-winning English fiction at the next table—I'm sitting in simply poncy Symposium with a glass of simply posh Chablis—were to ask, What are those books you have there beside you, I'd very much like to answer, A book of essays by Gunnar Ekelöf and a novel by some central European whose name almost certainly also means absolutely nothing to you, None of that silly scribbling you're on about, Which isn't to say of course that every central European novelist is worth anyone's attention. But they don't—The pilgrims' climb is a zigzag, which surely helps them up the steep inclines.

I'm trying to think of some kind of correspondence between the book and the bookmark but I can't. If there is one I can't put my finger on it. Unless it is quite deliberately a lack of correspondence so that the bookmark offers a repose from the book.

Another card is propped up against some spines, patiently awaiting its next book, which is quite appropriate given it is *Cat Looking at Fields at Asakusa* by Hiroshige. The white cat is hunched—that doesn't sound very comfortable but the cat looks very comfortable to me—on the windowsill, the window shoji open, of what must be an upper storey room, looking out through a type of lattice possibly peculiar to a pleasure house, over the fields and two cottages with Mount Fuji in the distance and in the sky in the middle distance a zigzag of avifauna.

Those are two postcards I like to use as bookmarks. A true paper one marks the novel I am reading by the central European. Detail of a lady preparing *The Tea Ceremony* by Eishi, with the complete picture in miniature on the back.

You might be forgiven for thinking that all my favourite bookmarks show images of Japan but they don't. Among others I like are a few bookstore giveaways. One, which is of the darkest unlaminated green, with a motif of a whirl above a block of lines is, or was, put out by a poetry bookshop, à tire-d'ailes. A quite unassuming one from Le Divan has become rather creased because the paper is too thin. Bookmarks made of paper and card do get worn at the edges but that only adds to the charm of having used them and of still using them. Another bookmark shows a detail of an ancient engraving. Two compositors and their printing press. While another is just elegant in the simplicity of its font on a laid paperboard.

But the leaf, the leaf fluttering down and landing and settling while you are reading, that's the loveliest bookmark of all. O life is sweet when all you need to sing is a bookmark.

I have overlooked a favourite business card—how could I—in two shades of brown, well, brown on apricoty, for Anzumura, Apricot Village, that's the translation, a café hidden away in a narrow alley close to the station in the Tokyo leafy city-suburb of Hino-Shi, which I often delight in using as a bookmark. It depicts a cat, one paw pours the coffee, the other paw holds a wafting cigarette, elbow on table, head supported, a sort of writer, or, thinker, about writing, a procrastinator. The artist is Jun Morioka. Although there is room here this procatinator is not depicted until the end piece. Just so.

"THIS TIME THE TEACHER SAID, each of you can write whatever comes to mind. To be honest, nothing comes to mind. I don't like this kind of freedom. I am happy to be tied to a set subject. I am too lazy to think of something myself. And what would it be? I'm equally happy to write about anything. I don't like hunting around for a topic." I know how he feels, fictional Fritz Kocher in Robert Walser's *A Schoolboy's Diary*—a title Walser gave to a non-Kocher story, not to a book—translated by Damion Searls (New York Review Books, 2013). I am just grateful he has got me off to a start here.

If there is one other book in particular I am glad I have recently got hold of it is the more than 2500 bible-paper page *Zibaldone: The Notebooks of Leopardi* translated into English, complete for the first time, by various hands (New York, Farrar, Straus and Giroux; & London, Penguin, 2013) under the auspices of the Leopardi Centre, University of Birmingham. Let me get my animadversions out of the way first because, by and large, it makes for beautiful reading: there is the more-often-than-not redundant or improvable *as to*, presumably thought, erroneously, to be a necessary prep, or an indicator of eloquence; a *which* and a *that* ripe for attention; the ubiquitous modern cheapskate glued, instead of signature sewn, hardback binding, rather as if it were just about holding together an expendable temporary work of reference. At least it easily opens flat.

A reference work, unpublished in Leopardi's lifetime, it certainly is—words, love, love of words, youth, age, death, animality, woman, yoman or noman (my coinage), society, history, politics, philosophy, science, arts, music, poetry, the past, the present, the future—but not temporary, not expendable. Any idea one cares to think of, along with quite a few one probably would not get around to thinking of, gets discussed, argued, within the more than 4500 pages of Leopardi's original notebooks. I do not understand everything I am reading. And why not. I am still learning. This monumental work is not one to begin at the beginning and read through to the end. It is to dip into, to page back and forth, to immerse oneself in, to come up for air, and to think. The editorial apparatus includes a bibliography of Leopardi's sources, his own 1827 subject index for his private use, and Michael Caesar and Franco D'Intino's comprehensive subject index.

I cannot add a thing to this huge undertaking which is why this hardly-antonym is short. What an excuse. Fritz Kocher: "Writing is about getting quietly worked up. Anyone who can't sit still but who always has to act loud and self-important to get his work done will never be able to write anything lively and beautiful. [. . .] Writing something thoughtful is good, but wanting to stuff your work too full of thoughts is something you should avoid." A pupil's wisdom, fictional or not.

Gunnar Ekelöf's Table

"One of the most important things in all art: leave a respectable part up to the reader, the observer, the listener, the participant. There shall be an empty setting at the ready-laid table. It is his." I like this, notwithstanding that Ekelöf provided some, sometimes contradictory, cues as well as more or less authorizing explications by others.

It is difficult to say categorically whether Ekelöf has been well-served in English. I would come down on the side of occasionally partly so. Occasionally, not only because of the variable quality of the translations and their presentation but because I believe nothing of the poetry is currently in print. The most visible book was *Selected Poems* (1971) translated by W H Auden and Leif Sjöberg, published in England in the Penguin Modern European Poets series and in the USA by Pantheon. As with every major collaboration between these two (the others are Dag Hammarskjöld and Pär Lagerkvist) stern warnings have to be sounded.

I would say that the best translations are those by Robert Bly and Christina Paulston, *Late Arrival on Earth* (Rapp & Carroll, 1967), aka *I Do Best Alone at Night* (Charioteer, 1968), expanded in Bly's *Friends, You Drank Some Darkness: Three Swedish Poets* (Beacon, 1975); Muriel Rukeyser and Leif Sjöberg's always difficult to find *Selected Poems* (Twayne, 1967), and *A Mölna Elegy* (Unicorn, 1984); and Rika Lesser's complete version of *Guide to the Underworld* (Univ. Massachusetts, 1980). I want to stress "complete" because it is the third volume of a trilogy, deeply Orientalist in nature, in particular Persian and Byzantine, of which Auden–Sjöberg's publishers present the first two volumes incompletely, though they have necessary equal integrity.

The second most visible translation would be Leonard Nathan and James Larson's *Songs of Something Else* (1982) but, oh dear, as so often with Princeton's attractive authoritative-looking Lockert Library of Poetry in Translation volumes, something here is immediately wrong—in this case typographical design getting the better of sense and sensitivity. The first line of every poem in both the Swedish and the English (the only bilingual Ekelöf there is) is indented. Why? Ekelöf has no such indents. I wrote a book in which each poem's first line (single word lines as it happens) is intentionally indented. What would it be except rubbish for an editor to decide that those lines should not be indented or that all my poems wherever they are should have their first lines indented.

Again, what is wrong with the presentation by Auden–Sjöberg? Ekelöf uses punctuation sparingly. In particular, he uses full stops at the ends of poems, almost never within lines and never at all at the ends of any but those last lines. Auden–Sjöberg's versions respect that but significantly mess it all up because their each and every line begins with a capital letter. Ekelöf may not have used full stops but he did make deliberate, meaningful use of when a line begins with a capital letter and when lines, the majority, do not. So the two most visible translations are those that are the most compromised. The opposite intermeddling occurs in, for example, Jonathan Galassi's much vaunted version of Leopardi's *Canti*, in which Leopardi's upper case beginnings to all his lines are reduced to, a supposedly modernist, I suppose, lower case—by this I mean I must assume that Auden preferred to obliterate one of Ekelöf's modernist aspects. If the reader thinks these are nothing but small niceties, think again, think of what it means, so to speak, to be an interfered-with poem.

For all his interest in Old Icelandic, why Sjöberg was so keen to let Auden get his grubby hands on Swedish poetry is a matter for conjecture, even if an obvious one. But it didn't work. Hammarskjöld's nomination of Auden did not persuade the Nobel committee—the irony being that Auden had produced a widely disseminated quite odious introduction to his injurious translation of Hammarskjöld's *Vägmärken*.

I cannot imagine either that Auden much liked Ekelöf's work and I doubt that Ekelöf's translation of a few Audens was more than a courtesy. Do not forget, Ekelöf also translated Eliot, not because he cared for the work—he really did not and he rightly strenuously resisted efforts by others to place him in Eliot's debt—but in order to come to some sort of terms with it. What too is to be made of Auden's shabby bitching at Ekelöf's home surroundings, the grandeur of the family's antique furniture, inherited but also life-earned? As if the poet, in the very fact, act, of being a poet, forfeits rights to assume a decent wealth and comfort even and whether or not in the face of a painful exit.

There are other books by and about Ekelöf worth seeking out. *Modus Vivendi: Selected Prose* (Norvik, 1996)—a shame that translator Erik Thygesen's introduction takes up almost a third of this in-print book in place of more Ekelöf prose; Leif Sjöberg's *A Reader's Guide to Gunnar Ekelöf's A Mölna Elegy* (Twayne, 1973)—a somewhat, despite Ekelöf's empty setting at the table, indispensible, if over-egged, companion to the aforementioned translation with Muriel Rukeyser, which took another ten years to find book publication; and Ross Shideler's brief study, in a Modern Philology series, *Voices Under the Ground: Themes and Images in the Early Poetry of Gunnar Ekelöf* (Univ. California, 1973), which also includes translation.

The best Swedish edition of Ekelöf's works, out of print but quite easily found, complete or volume by volume, is the eight-volume annotated *Skrifter* (1991), edited for Bonniers by Reidar Ekner, the first three volumes of which contain the most important poetry collections. For the English-speaking reader who would like to delve deeper into a brilliant intellect, by turns mysterious and open, in which journeys into the classical and the real, the ancient and the modern, into the dark and the light, arrive at reconciliations, it is not that difficult to grasp a modern Scandinavian language.

The opening quotation from Ekelöf, in Inger Ekelöf's foreword to *En röst* [A Voice] (1973), is found in the heading to the notes by Rika Lessar in her translation of *Guide to the Underworld*.

All the translations of the poetry pre-date *Skrifter*, which means they are based on editions that do not show Ekelöf's final amendments. This accounts for a few discrepancies. For example, Ekelöf cancelled the last line, "Your time is Water. I am your water-clock.", given in *Guide to the Underworld*.

There was an academic printing of *A Molnä Elegy* before it appeared as a separate book: in *Comparative Criticism Yearbook*, 1 (CUP, 1979).

For a discussion of Hammarskjöld and Auden–Sjöberg see Kaj Feldman in the *Times Literary Supplement* (10 September 1999), and ensuing correspondence. For a discussion of Lagerkvist and Auden–Sjöberg see Anthony Barnett, trans., in Pär Lagerkvist, *Evening Land* (Allardyce Book, 2001), repr. with corrections in Anthony Barnett, *Translations* (Tears in the Fence, in assoc. Allardyce Book ABP, 2012).

A DISACCUMULATION OF KNOWLEDGE

THE WRITING I AM DOING AT THE MOMENT HAS A SUBTITLE, which begins: "A Disaccumulation of Knowledge". I know perfectly well that there is nothing original in that but even so I have been caught by surprise. Clarice Lispector is a writer I have often thought of reading but I have not done so until now for not very sensible reasons, including endorsements by certain commentators who arouse my suspicion, though I shall not include perhaps her staunchest advocate, Hélène Cixous, among them.

Thanks to a new friend, whose judgement I can listen to, I have found out I was wrong. Lispector is a writer I now know I wanted to read ages ago. At least, it is a pleasure to have found her at last and to immerse myself in courageous, fierce, gentle, beautiful works of fibs and truth, fairy tale and reality. Lispector has simples for her philosophic and parabolic complexities. Disconcerting changes in direction unexpectedly but then oh so obviously straighten out. Momentary detours that turn out not to have been detours at all.

In one of her numerous Saturday newspaper features, the *Crônicas*, in which she had carte blanche to write about anything she wanted, to write anything she wanted, Lispector quotes Thoreau: "It is only when we discard all knowledge that we begin to know." So there you are.

In "The Making of a Novel" Lispector writes: "As I write them down, I am convinced once more that, however paradoxical it may sound, the greatest drawback about writing is that one has to use words. It is a problem. For I should prefer a more direct form of communication, that tacit understanding one often finds between people. If I could write by carving on wood or by stroking a child's head or strolling in the countryside, I would never resort to using words. I would do what so many people do who are not writers, and with the same joy and torment as those who write, and with the same bitter disappointments which are beyond consolation. I would live and no longer use words. And this might be the solution. And as such, be most welcome."

I dare say this is too much of a protest because in her cut-short life—
she died of ovarian cancer at the age of fifty-six—Lispector wrote an
abundance of novels, short stories and essays. That does not proscribe the
expression of her sentiment, nor is it to say that writing came to her easily
(her characters also say enough for us to believe that, in the ways that she
wanted, it did not: "I don't know what I'm writing about: I am obscure to
myself." "This is the word of someone who cannot."—*Água Viva*) but I am
going to assume that she would not approve of others using it to justify
sparseness—something I would like to do. But I won't. It's as if I would
like to stay in her good books. Though it is not certain that in the bons
mots of that idiomatic expression I can because my subtitle continues:
"Being Nothing More than Drafts and Fragments That, Not Which, Are
Not Enough". But I do admit to that Not Enough.

This is a time of renewed interest in Lispector in the English-speaking
world—my writing about her here is what is called a coincidence—with a
reissue programme by New Directions and Penguin Books of some novels and *Complete Stories*, in new translations, from the Brazilian Portuguese,
and Benjamin Moser's all-embracing biography *Why This World*. Regretta-
bly, the posthumous novel *A Breath of Life*, translated for the first time, is
marred by a cringe-making exchange between Moser and Almodóvar.

Discovering the World, Lispector's near complete *Crónicas*, translated by
Giovanni Pontiero, was published by Carcanet in 1992. It is long out of
print but about two thirds were reissued in 1996 by New Directions as
Selected Crónicas. This is still in print though it would not surprise if a new
translation is in the offing. I am coming to the end of those pieces, which
I would rather did not end, so to assuage my disappointment, though I
still have novels to read, I shall continue writing those insufficient drafts
and fragments of mine, obliged to accept that almost certainly I cannot
turn them into an abundance. But what, apart from words, or leaving them
alone, can be my justification? Inertia? Faint-heartedness? Dreaminess?

Remembering how I would rest my weary head on my weary arms on
the desk—the school desk then, later the table—in the afternoons . . .

Lispector proposes the antithesis of "I can remember nothing of before I am born", the opening sentence of a novel (title undisclosed) I tried to write in my twenties but couldn't. I am finding it difficult to leave this Antonym alone. I am going to stop and not look at it again.

FELISBERTO HERNÁNDEZ

Taking note of what Lispector has to say has led me to a another remarkable writer I would probably otherwise not have found, the Uraguayan Felisberto Hernández, who was also a self-taught concert pianist. Stories translated into English are *Piano Stories* (Marsilio, 1993; New Directions, 2014) and *Lands of Memory* (New Directions, 2002, 2013). His mysterious compositions are played by Sergio Elena at www.felisberto.org.uy

The sake cup

A Sake Cup

USUALLY, IN FACT UP TILL NOW NOT AT ALL, I do not publish what I call my Antonyms in a review of which I am an editor. These so-called Antonyms first appeared, the first six, in a journal of the English Association *The Use of English*. When its then editor, known to readers of *Snow*, departed he took on the role of reviews editor at *Tears in the Fence*. My Antonyms followed. With one exception, "The Publisher", that is where they have been appearing ever since. I write them for nothing—I wish it were otherwise because writing should be paid for even if it isn't—because I am allowed to write whatever I wish, without editorial meddling in such matters as punctuation. This is not trivial. It is important. Anyway, this sake cup of mine is a different kettle of fish, a different cup of sake, altogether. It might be that it should not be called an Antonym at all because I think it is a wholly positive piece, free of oppositional contradictions.

＊

"Form"—"It was an iron sake flask. There was a moment when this thread pattern flask taught him the beauty of 'form'." These beautiful lines make a complete section of *A Fool's Life* by Akutagawa Ryūnosuke. The Japanese word for this thread pattern is itome. It might be that the translation should simply read "itome flask". I would like to think that I have experienced a similar, quiet eureka moment.

This happened while I was staying with my companion, without whose help I could not have translated *A Fool's Life*, in a beautiful traditional house a stone's throw from the sea a short wintery pine-clad hill drive from Kanazawa on the Noto Peninsular. One day we took a bus and a local train that ran beside water meadows with herons to meet a friend in nearby Wajima, a city famous for inventing a unique method of lacquerware production, Wajima-nuri, in the Ishikawa Prefecture of the snowy Hokuriku region. But this is not about lacquerware.

Strolling in Wajima's daily Morning Market, a low-roofed street filled with stalls and stores of all kinds, we entered a small pottery shop, doors open wide on to the street. The shelves displayed sake flasks and cups and other ware, greyish, metal-looking, which I picked up and put down, examining them in a sheepish effort to look for all the world as if I knew what I was doing, before I decided to settle on the one I wanted to buy.

This most modest unostentatious cup came with a paper slip, I have managed not to lose it, explaining the history and characteristics of this ware, which my companion has translated. Here it is adapted.

*

History recounts that a variety of pottery was in production for four hundred years, beginning in the Heian period, around the tenth to eleventh centuries, lasting into the Muromachi period, around the fourteenth century, in a small village named Suzu, located at the north-eastern most tip of the Noto Peninsula. This pottery was used for everyday ware over quite a large area, to the north of, and to the far north of, the Kansai region, centred in Kyoto. The pottery was produced in large quantities and transported as far as Hokkaidō by the famous convoy ships bearing the name Kitamaebune, which followed the route along the Sea of Japan. Suddenly, during the Sengoku period, the age of Japan's civil wars, around 1400–1600, the pottery disappeared and came to be known as ancient phantom or rare pottery ware.

In the mid 1950s the kiln remains at Suzu were excavated, to widespread attention. Archaeologists and historical researchers named the pottery Suzu-yaki, Suzu ware. In Shōwa 53, 1978, after the long sleep of four hundred years, the restored kiln at Suzu was relit for firing. Since then, the number of Suzu kiln houses and masters of the special skills required has steadily increased. It is curious that four hundred years of production was followed by four hundred years of sleep.

*

Suzu ware is characterized by a simplicity, taken over from the skills found in Japanese Sue pottery, brought to Japan from the Continent, the Korean Peninsula, by Korean potters in the mid Tumulus period, around the fifth century. It uses the soil around Suzu, containing a high proportion of iron, to which a very high temperature is applied, more than 1200° celsius. The pottery is unglazed in a method called kusube-yaki, smoked out. The iron in the soil, combining with the carbon, produces a sombre beauty of grey-black colour. The ash from the burnt logs works to cover the pottery in a natural glaze of delicate tones known as hai-katsugi, ash-covered. Over the years, the more regularly it is used, this yaki jime sekki, pottery fired fiercely at high temperature, takes on a most harmonious texture. It is best not to hide it away in a cupboard but to keep it out on the cup board with the sake.

*

I handed the cup I wanted to buy to the shopkeeper, I think he was wearing spectacles, who turned it in his hand, smiling approvingly, saying "You have made a very good choice." Like the modest earthenware holy grail in that film. Well, I have to admit that I felt rather pleased with myself, even if that is not as modest.

NOTE

Akutagawa Ryūnosuke, *A Fool's Life*, trans. Anthony Barnett and Toraiwa Naoko (Allardyce Book, 2007), repr. with corrections in Anthony Barnett, *Translations* (Tears in the Fence, in assoc., Allardyce Book ABP, 2012)

FANTASTIC, FANTASTICAL

WHAT DO VENICE AND THE NETHERLANDS HAVE IN COMMON, in particular? Do not aspects of their survival depend on their ways with water? I am struck by two large format books of visual images. Of course I am not literally struck because they have not fallen off the shelf where they are lying flat, I have taken them down. In the back of my mind I have often thought that an Antonym on both books together was somehow to be got at, I had made a note to do it, out of the water, I now understand, so to speak, but I couldn't get at it before.

In *Living Venice* Andrea Zanzotto contributes an introductory essay to colour photographs, most in landscape format, by Fulvio Roiter, whose origins, like Zanzotto's, lie in the Veneto. In *Unbuilt Netherlands* Cees Nooteboom contributes a commentary, tracked throughout the book, on visionary projects, designs, drawings, sketches, paintings, but of course no photographs, by architects dating back to the mid-nineteenth century. The editors explain: "the book contains designs that never got further than the drawing board because they were too fantastical, too advanced, or impractical for technical, financial or political reasons." Contrary books, so suited to an Antonym, both out-of-their-ordinary, though there has never been anything ordinary about either of these poets, quite different in their work, though I think both classicists at heart in their modernity, whatever else someone may wish to make of Zanzotto's apparent avant-gardisms, in all but his earliest work, and their psychologies. About that, Nooteboom has always been a wide-awake traveller. It is one of the ways in which he identifies himself. Whereas Zanzotto, for the last however-many-years of his life, felt quite unable to set foot outside the town of his beloved Veneto. So I count myself fortunate to have met him in England.

Nooteboom opens with: "The essence of a never-built building is that it isn't there. It is invisible because it doesn't exist. No one can live in it, no one can walk past it, no one can clean it, no one will be able to remember it, because it has never existed. An unborn child will never change the world, an unwritten book will never make us think, the unpainted picture will never be photographed." Of course, that is not the whole story: "What this book shows is what the Netherlands *could* have looked like, but also, and this is the breath-taking paradox, what it *did* look like. The unbuilt forms part of a culture just as much as the built, it exists as thought, as response, as idea, as wish."

Zanzotto opens with: "Venice, maybe: Only someone with long experience of taking journeys, tearing up roots and deliberately breaking down settled attitudes and habits could induce in themselves the kind of state suitable for seeing the places in these photographs. And even then he ought, by rights, to approach them as people used to before technological times—across the marshes, by canal, over fields, gliding along in boats piloted with necessary caution until all of a sudden the old distinctions between things as we know them begin to be doubted and the world seems topsy-turvy for a moment as we come on domes, roofs, huts emerging from the watery nothingness as if their legs had sunk deep into shifting sands and great clods of vegetable sucking power, after a headlong fall out of the infinite spaces [. . .] Only this kind of spirit, it seems, walking or swimming or plodding through water from Portogruaro down towards Venice, could prepare us for such an unexpected germination of the real and the fantastic."

So you see, Cees, Andrea is speaking to you. And, Andrea, Cees is speaking to you. The fantastic realized, the fantastical unrealized. What, apart from the seemingly obvious, might be the difference? "The circle, our long circumambulation that started at Galman's bridge over the IJ and ends with Benthem's Rijnmond Tower, is complete. The long discussion, the vehement arguments, die down and silence returns to the great city of never-built buildings. I imagine I am alone now, I imagine that for once, very briefly, these buildings   "

One may not find these books easily. They are out of print, at least in English. But if you are moved by ways with water, byways by water, by cit-

[59]

ies, by what poets get up to when they are not really out-of-their-ordinary, do seek them out.

NOTE

Cees Nooteboom, *Unbuilt Netherlands: Visionary Projects by Berlage, Oud, Duiker, Van den Broek, Van Eyck, Hertzberger and Others*, trans. Adrienne Dixon (London, Architectural Press, 1985), original Dutch eds., *Nooit gebouwd Nederland* (1980, 1983). In a new bilingual German and Dutch ed., *Nie gebaute Niederlande* (2000), Nooteboom elaborates on Walter Benjamin and the flâneur.

Fulvio Roiter, text Andrea Zanzotto, *Living Venice*, trans. Maurice Rowdon (Udine, Magnus, 1978), original Italian ed., *Essere Venezia* (1977). A second English ed., *Venice* (London, Thames & Hudson, 1979), is deprecated because Zanzotto's introductory essay is replaced, it really doesn't matter by whom.

Nooteboom has his own book about Venice, in German translation only: *Venezianische Vignetten* (Berlin, Insel, 2013), not as complete as he would like it to be so he is writing another one.

Extracts from correspondence between Nooteboom and AB appear in *Snow lit rev*, 3 (spring 2015).

Three Short Antonyms

On this sunny today I am doing the rounds of the town's gardens, cafés and the loose tea shop and tasting bar except the loose tea shop and tasting bar is closed today because today is a Monday, and a holiday too, so instead I drop in on some friends for a tea, to try to write because I cannot stuck at home although I have gone back home to type this up a bit. The stone is warm where I am sitting. The stone was warm where I was sitting.

Faces in the Crowd

Joshua Owen is a real Mexican poet, living in New York in 1928. Why should I expect Gilberto Zvorsky to be a real poet too. I feel quite stupid checking out www to see if anything is posted there about him. I know perfectly well he is one of Valeria Luiselli's conceits. I have mixed up their names. Gilberto Owen. Joshua Zvorsky. That's better. From the first mention of these faces in the crowd it is obvious that Zvorsky, author of *That*, translator of Owen, is Louis Zukofsky. The more one enters the past and present obfuscations of this bonbon of a novel the clearer that, indeed all, becomes. The question I have to ask myself is why Zvorsky when all Owen, Williams, Dickinson, Pound, Lorca, Langston Hughes, half a dozen others, for example, Beckett, Wittgenstein, not to mention Duke Ellington, are checked with their real names even though their conversations, or the conversations about them, take place only in Valeria Luiselli's imagination.

I shall start over again. New York resident Mexican Valeria Luiselli has written a bonbon of a novel in which a thinly disguised Louis Zukofsky, Joshua Zvorsky, engages with Mexican poet Gilberto Owen and Federico García Lorca. It is alternately set in the present, in which Luiselli searches for traces of Owen, and 1928 Harlem, where Luiselli finds him, along with impossible glimpses of Pound. Owen, Zvorsky, Lorca visit a bar and floor show. Ellington is playing piano. Lorca brags "The Duke and I are big buddies." Which is about, I was about to say objective, as subjective as you can get. Valeria Luiselli, *Faces in the Crowd*, trans. Christina MacSweeney (London, Granta, 2013; Minneapolis, Coffee House, 2014).

Trans-Atlantyk

"WE CONSIDER OUR TRANSLATION EXPERIMENTAL. We have devised it in order to bring *Trans-Atlantyk* to as many English-speaking readers as will bear with it, even like it. We hope that ours will not be the last translation of this unique and important work." It cannot be that often that a translator actively invites future translations. That is what Carolyn French and Nina Karsov do with their 1994 Yale University Press version of Witold Gombrowicz's guffaw of a novel. Their wish has been fulfilled with the same publisher's 2014 *Trans-Atlantyk: An Alternate Translation* by Danuta Borchardt: "Witold Gombrowicz deemed *Trans-Atlantyk* his most untranslatable work, and it will always be a great challenge to any translator. When I read Carolyn French and Nina Karsov's translation, I felt that another attempt was justified." I cannot be sure but I think I detect an absence of reciprocal humility from Borchardt, whether or not she may have good reason from a literary point of view. I do not myself shy away from barbed criticisms of other translators so I think Borchardt tries to affect a little too much subtlety with her slant of a barb. Not content simply to present her own version a straight talking onslaught would not have been a bad thing.

This is not a review so I am not obliged to assail you my reader with the proper stuff of reviews and I shall not do so. Gombrowicz wrote *Trans-Atlantyk* when he found himself stranded, and among the Polish expatriate community, in Buenos Aires at the outbreak of World War II, in and as a parody of an old Polish literary genre, the gawęda, in imitation of manor house fireside chats. Both translations seek to replicate this by drawing on examples of unconventional and ribald English authors of the past.

The curious thing is that, as a keen consumer of Gombrowicz since his works first began to appear in English, *Trans-Atlantyk* is the one work I have not managed to get to grips with until now. This means that I find Borchardt's version to be, loathsome word, accessible, more accessible, apparently, than French–Karsov's. This is what has happened: I have French–Karsov's version upstairs and Borchardt's downstairs and in my pocket when I leave the house. I have taken to reading the same passages alternately in both versions and at last I can make sense of French–Karsov's. Unfortunately, my part Polish and Lithuanian ancestry offers in itself absolutely no insight into which should be the preferred translation. Borchardt bases her version on Gombrowicz's 1957 revision while French–Karsov's is based on the 1953 serialization as it first appeared in a literary journal. Neither translation gives a clue to what the differences are. I am also a bit miffed to discover that translations of other Gombrowicz novels I have lived with for years in blissful innocence have also been replaced, behind my back as it were, by new Borchardt translations. This isn't always fun.

THE YOUTH OF THINGS

KAJII MOTOJIRŌ (JAPANESE NAME ORDER) was the author of a small but significant body of short stories with essay-like qualities. He died of tuberculosis in 1932 at the age of thirty-one. Until now the only work of his really known in English, through being anthologized, has been his very first story "Lemon", in which for a moment he toys with the idea that the lemon he has left atop a stack of art books he has built in the famous Maruzen store is an exploding bomb. Stephen Dodd, lecturer in Japanese at London University's SOAS, has put things right with *The Youth of Things: Life and Death in the Age of Kajii Motojirō* (University of Hawaii Press, 2014). The first half of this generous book consists of chapters relating specifically to that title: "Illness as Empowerment", "Modernism and Its Endings", "Things of Beauty", "The Subject of Change". The second half of the book consists of translations of eighteen of Kajii's output of twenty finished stories, which read as beautifully in English as I must imagine they do in Japanese. Dodd's topical analysis is revealing and very helpful, though how I wish he could have done without citing a couple of academic commentators, on matters outside Japanese studies, the very sight of whose names raises my particular hackles. That's my problem. But in this respect there is absolutely no reason, apart from the vagaries of publishers, why Dodd's translations of Kajii's stories should not find a wider general readership with their own dedicated publication. They are worth it.

The word beauty is both apposite and troubled. Kajii's anecdotes and descriptions are suffused with the disclosure of a personal psychology, juxtaposing the beauty of the things he sees or senses around him, often in the most unexpected incidents and settings, with the bodily and mental disturbance of acute sensitivity to illness and looming death—imagined corpses buried under a cherry tree seeming for the narrator to be what give rise to the cherry's blossoms is but one example. Yet lest I give a wrong impression, even in the darkest moments, when the light, from the sun or an electric bulb, has all but faded, it is an at least potentially restorative mood rather than morbidity that the reader of these stories is most often left to contemplate. "'To sit here like this until the sun goes down, what magnificent hopelessness that is,' I thought. 'They're waiting for me at the inn with dinner ready, completely unaware. As for me, I don't have a clue what tonight will bring.'"

Among a number of European avant-garde artists with whom Kajii is known to have been familiar is Kandinsky. Kandinsky's colour lithograph "Kleine Welten 1", dated 1922, on Japanese paper, depicts an explosion of yellow, red, blue, green and black curves, oblongs and scimitar shapes. Dodd resists the temptation to suggest that this might have been the inspiration for Kajii's exploding "Lemon" among the art, written two years later, but in a sublime stroke of associative presentation he does reproduce it on the lemon yellow dust jacket of *The Youth of Things*.

WHENEVER I SIT DOWN TO WRITE there is likely to be a disturbance, if not of my own making then elsewhere. This Sunday it is the barely interrupted noise from a power saw off in the distance but close enough to oblige me to do all I can to avoid using it as an excuse not to write. Barely interrupted rain keeps me inside, and to hell with screen distractions, so a few lines are possible. I rest in the knowledge that the one with the power must be getting drenched.

It is no secret that I often cite and sing the praises of novelist and travel chronicler Cees Nooteboom. Ever since I first read *A Song of Truth and Semblance* I find more often than not his sentences and thinking mesmerizing. "The lion, sprawling on his lawn, has dispensed with the world; he sleeps within his own coat of arms." What an observation, in the "Zoo", in Buenos Aires, in *Letters to Poseidon*, which ranges far and wide through myth, fact, history, experience, imagination. Toward the end of the book, "Poseidon xxII" opens with a confession. Now I understand in a new light how this writer works, though it is a light that on reflection must always have been clear: "I have a condition that I call tumbling thoughts, a state of confusion that sends me spinning from one thought to another." There is a tortoise "whom I recognise by his markings. He is a member of the nobility, he bears his own coat of arms. He knows me too and has decided I am harmless, even though I am trespassing on his property. As soon as I see him, the thoughts begin to tumble, and I walk over to him. He raises his old philosopher's head and, looking up into the sun, tries to gauge my size. He does not seem disappointed, I recognise that expression on his face, a form of satisfaction linked to the fact that Achilles has once again been unable to catch up with him. And then another tumble and I am with Achilles," and if I do not stop quoting I shall end up with the whole book.

One thing that sets Nooteboom apart is that his lovely fearless thoughts tumble through his pen straight onto the page, apparently effortlessly, though I cannot know whether that is really true, in a state of confusion—but I don't believe it—or not. My own tumbling thoughts are more likely than not to stay stuck in my head. That's also to do with spiritness. Spiritedness. Not faint-heartedness. Osip Mandelstam had those tumbling thoughts too with the spirit of the pen, or the pencil: "Thus an anecdote in his mouth sounded like a theorem. A general runs through all the dishes on a menu, rejects them all, and exclaims: 'What filth!' A student who had overheard the general's remark asks him to name the various ranks of the government service and when he has finished, exclaims: 'Is that all? What filth!'"

NOTE

Cees Nooteboom, *Letters to Poseidon*, trans. Laura Watkinson (Maclehose, 2014)

Osip Mandelstam, "The Noise of Time", in *The Noise of Time*, trans. Clarence Brown (North Point, 1986; Quartet, 1988)

SETTLED BY DOVES

THIS SNOW LEAF IS SETTLED BY DOVES, NOT CENTAURS, the latter being *Snow*'s, indeed ABP's generally, preferred house font. Dear Centaur, whether you are male or female, do not chastise me for abandoning you to take shape for a moment in a different flight of fancy. You are not so far apart in that you both have the oblique e-stroke I like, whatever your other Venetian Jenson serif derived differences may be, indeed are. Quite. You Doves are remarkably grounded considering your escapades—to put it muddily mildly—in The Thames, while you Centaur are quite, how shall I put it, escapably, escapadably, fleet of foot.

Here in a nutshell is the infamous famous story. A century ago, the partners in the Doves Press, Thomas Cobden-Sanderson and Emery Walker, fell out. From 1916, over three years of nights, Cobden-Sanderson consigned the complete fount, punches, matrices and metal, to its watery grave off the Hammersmith Bridge so that no one would ever again be able to print books in his beautiful 16pt type, cut by Edward Prince. In 2013, Robert Green of Typespec, Manchester, revived the Doves Press Roman in a digital facsimile, based on original books and ephemera. Not content, in 2014 Green embarked on an expedition with Port of London Authority divers, recovering a portion of the lost metal. In early 2015 he reissued the type in a more precise version, which is, mostly, what you are reading here. Why mostly?* The original Doves Type was roman only, without italic or small caps. Typespec's release is true to that, while adding some new glyphs and diacritics. When Doves Press printed in italic it used Edinburgh foundry Miller & Richard Old Style. No digital so-called Old Style italic fits at all satisfactorily with Doves.

Assiduous research reveals that Swedish typographer Torbjörn Olsson designed and issued a version of Doves Type in 1994–1995, evidently updated 2002, based on his study of Doves Press print. Olsson is hard to track down: email addresses bounce back; the Swedish firm T4 through which a few of his

* Distinct features of Doves Type include dropped opening " 'quotes' ", and curtailed ʃ and markedly offset i tittle, both true to 1470 Jenson, absent or attenuated in almost all revivals and derivations

types are sold does not list Doves. What is more, The Doves Type® is now a name registered by Typespec. Don't ask me how but I have got hold of Olsson's version. If it was the only Doves revival in existence it would be good but Green's, Green's first version even, is more faithful and better proportioned, the more so in light of studying original metal—in the roman. Where Olsson's version comes into its own is in his inclusion of newly designed italic and small caps, and alternate lining figures also not present in the original or in Green—see the figure 4 in the bottom line of the previous page—with some new glyphs and ornaments, to accompany his roman. The first line, and *Snow* and ABP, in the second line of the previous page, and now here, are set in Olsson's version, in adjusted pointing. To have a more than reasonable accompanying *italic*—see also below—is a boon. To forego SMALL CAPS digitally generated from roman for true SMALL CAPS so designed is useful too.

Thank you, Centaur, an olive branch

NOTE

Typespec The Doves Type® *has roman discretionary ligature ct*
http://www.typespec.co.uk/doves-type/
http://www.typespec.co.uk/doves-type-revival/
http://www.typespec.co.uk/recovering-the-doves-type/

Olsson Doves Type Pro *has roman & italic discretionary ligatures ct & st*
http://home.swipnet.se/~w-10011/Tobbe/Tobbe.html
http://luc.devroye.org/fonts-27212.html

Marianne Tidcombe, *The Doves Press* (London, British Library, & New Castle, DE, Oak Knoll, 2002 [2003]), comprehensive history, set in Galliard CC, a non-oblique-e type first issued 1978, based on 16th-c. Granjon
Simon Garfield, *Just My Type: A Book About Fonts* (London, Profile, 2010), 90–94, chap. "Doves", lay account

Bruce Rogers, *Paragraphs on Printing: Elicited from Bruce Rogers in Talks with James Hendrickson on the Functions of the Book Designer* (New York, Rudge, 1943; fascimile repr. New York, Dover, 1979), *c.*100 illus., set in 1932 MT recut of 1788, then 1930 MT, Bell, a non-oblique-e type used by Rogers at the Riverside Press in 1900
Bruce Rogers, *The Centaur Types* (Chicago, October, 1949; facsimile repr. West Lafayette, IN, Purdue Univ., 1996), illus. account of the type, first cut 1914, recut 1929 MT; Rogers visited England 1916, the year Doves Type began to meet its fate, working first with Doves' Emery Walker, then as advisor to CUP, 1917–1919
Joseph Blumenthal, *Bruce Rogers: A Life in Letters, 1870–1957* (Austin, TX, Taylor, 1989)
Jerry Kelly, & Misha Beletsky, *The Noblest Roman: A History of the Centaur Types of Bruce Rogers* (Rochester, NY, RIT, 2015), incl. new research into unpublished papers

The dove ornaments above are two of several in black & white in Olsson Doves Type Pro
The olive branch is from the Author

Two Childlike Antonyms

Lost Things

On just one winter's day walk i come across two different woolly gloves and a woolly hat. From their sizes they all belong to children. They lie on the pavement or have been placed on a fence by a considerate passer-by. They remind me of some childish losses. A raggedy but cuddly for me toy dog dragged to the refuse bin from grievously protesting hands. I am not ready for this. A colourful beach bucket washed out to sea. I watched it sinking with the water spilling over its rim. My model sailing boat bobbing off the coast. I do wonder to where it sailed. Later, the rosewood bell of a beloved clarinet. But that was found again. A considerate passer-by had placed it on a post. So then, not every loss is a set-up for later human losses.

Don't-Mean-a-Things and Will-Be-Dones

What do you never miss on the telly? Having repeated that far from pleasing contraction I might as well go for mag too. So I read this question in a mag. And I looked for the answer expecting to read about the programme the interviewee couldn't care less about seeing. This is not the first time I have understood clearly intended meaning for its opposite, though which is the logic and which the illogic I am still hard put to say. The Ellington–Mills song "It Don't Mean a Thing, if It Ain't Got that Swing" seemed just as well to mean it doesn't matter, if it doesn't swing. All my teen passion for jazz wasn't enough to convince me that it couldn't possibly be so frivolous even as I didn't believe it. I learn that these are examples of *amphiboly* or *amphibology*. But I shall call them *don't-mean-a-things*. (If you) starve a cold, (you will) feed a fever. The dawning that the Fifth of November celebrated the failure to blow up Parliament, not the attempt to blow it up, was a childhood puzzle. After all, why, in shop doorways and on street corners, are we asked to give a penny for this guy? Yes, I know he is going to burn too. And what of Thy Will be done, as I heard it at morning assembly. Who was this Will? How and why would he be done? Though it was vaguer than that. That's a *will-be-done*. Then——, My body lies over the ocean. What! So what could be wrong with me, or my eyes and ears, or my wits? Or meaningful fairy tales.

A POSTCARD FOR TAKASHI HIRAIDE

THERE ARE MOMENTS, many, when I feel as if I couldn't care less whether I ever walk into a bookshop again, not so much because of what might be there, which is daunting enough, but because of what is unlikely to be there. Yet here I am tapping away on my laptop in this small town's recently opened new bookshop, waterisitsname, except that it isn't so much of a bookshop as a coffee shop, good for tapping away in, with a large children's activity area.

But there you are, that's how I discovered the only "bestseller" I have come across in years that means very much to me: Takashi Hiraide's *The Guest Cat*. "The *New York Times* bestseller" the cover proudly proclaims. And indeed it is a wonderful tale, of Chibi, Little One, who changes the lives of the couple, and the house, she takes to. Ever since Sōseki's *I Am a Cat*—or, what would be better, given the noblesse expressed in the original, *I, A Cat*—it cannot be an easy thing to bring fine new feline qualities to a novel in Japanese, which is what Hiraide does.

As is my wont I sought out the other two books by Hiraide available in English. *For the Fighting Spirit of the Walnut* is a bilingual edition of one hundred and eleven unusual prose passages, more unusual, if I may say it, than my own *Etiquette in the City* aka "42 Passages". "*Juglans*, with our blind eyes and ringing ears, I am the one who is eternally distraught, shorn of all I have."—from 109. I suppose some would say surrealistic. Let them. What does it matter. At random: "Little sister. A common-law bolt of lightning, scattered clouds that move through the underpass. A distant fire deep in the heart, a keyhole made of light. The most impassive, most scathing, pearl."—102. "Getting off the train, there was only one exit to the north. I passed a quiet old commercial strip along the tracks, what seemed like a row of repeating liquor stores, grocery stores, and rice shops—in other words I took a long detour south around the station house. With someone leading the way, I was finally able to stand before the tree of my dreams."—25. Without giving too much away, for a significant thing happens in the final section, Sawako Nakayasu's preface explains that in Japanese "fighting spirit" and "walnut" both have double meanings: "fighting spirit / fibre"; "walnut / wrapping/enclosure". So I say this is also the brain. A doctrine of signatures. In the USA *Cat* and *Walnut* have the same publisher but would you believe it, of course, only *The Guest Cat* is published in the UK.

"In order to create a country, you have to create its mother tongue. In other words, unless a mother tongue comes into being, the country never will. [. . .] On the other hand, the name of a non-existent prince sometimes turns up in an already visible land. D. E.—the initials, as I was told, were, because of the big coffee firm Douwe Egberts, common on the streets of Holland, were they not?"—from May 15, 1987. Donald Evans was a one-off American painter who invented numerous countries for which he painted numerous one-off postage stamps and made cancellation marks. Some were one-offs, others were in thematic series. He was a friend to painters and poets. He died at the age of thirty-one in a fire in his Amsterdam apartment building. His life and work is documented in *The World of Donald Evans*. He was interviewed for *The Paris Review*. So I don't need to say much more here. In *Postcards to Donald Evans*, Hiraide goes to Europe and the USA in search of Evans's life—family, friends, locations. One trail leads to another, another to an impasse. There's a meeting with John Ashbery. Hiraide writes postcards on an almost daily basis, some one hundred and eighty-six in all, mostly unposted. Ten years later some forty are lost. Or did they reach Donald Evans? Hiraide visits Lundy, issuer of its own unofficial stamps, in homage to a trip Evans tried to make with his girlfriend, only to be thwarted on the one day they might have got there by rough seas cancelling the crossing.

I want to say Takashi Hiraide is a truly remarkable writer. He also publishes beautifully printed v wwalnut editions.

Takashi Hiraide in English: "On Kawara", trans. Kumiko Kiuchi, in *Snow lit rev*, 4 (spring 2016); *The Guest Cat*, trans. Eric Selland (New Directions, 2014; Picador, 2014); *For the Fighting Spirit of the Walnut*, trans. Sawako Nakayasu (New Directions, 2008); *Postcards to Donald Evans*, trans. Tomoyuki Iino (Tibor de Nagy, 2003). Website http://takashihiraide.com/

Willy Eisenhart, *The World of Donald Evans* (Harlin Quist, 1980)

If Douglas Oliver Read Natsume Sōseki

"Earlier, I mentioned three themes in my own poetry: death of the baby, of the old man or woman, and swift cruelties in which a slower knowledge arises. These seem like faces of time: time as a successsion of instants which are unfulfilled; time as a unity of what has passed and what is passing in the elderly's deaths—a life-full unity which has much to offer the future; and time as swiftly passing and cruel, bringing defeat and death." Douglas Oliver's "Three Lilies" describes different types of death. If it isn't an original idea it is nevertheless a most beautiful expression of it. I was brought up short on rereading this dialogue in Natsume Sōseki's *Kokoro*:

> I was somewhat comforted by Sensei's last remarks. Sensei watched me for a while, observing my relief, and then said:
> "But men are pretty helpless creatures, whether they are healthy or not. Who can say how they will die, or when?"
> "You, of all people, think this?"
> "Of course. I may be healthy, but that does not prevent me from thinking about death."
> Sensei smiled faintly.
> "Surely, there are many men who die suddenly, yet quietly, from natural causes. And then there are those whose sudden, shocking deaths are brought about by unnatural violence."
> "What do you mean by unnatural violence?"
> "I am not quite sure; but wouldn't you say that people who commit suicide are resorting to unnatural violence?"
> "Then I suppose you would say that people who are murdered die also through unnatural violence?"
> "I had never thought of that. But you are right, of course."

If Oliver read *Kokoro* it would have been in that translation. Now there is a more recent translation, which, I am assured, is closer to the voice of the original—though one could imagine it would be six of one and half a dozen of the other:

I felt somewhat comforted.

Seeing this change in me, Sensei added, "But sick or well, humans are fragile creatures, you know. There's no anticipating how and when they might die, or for what reason."

"That's how you feel yourself, is it, Sensei?"

"I'm in fine health, but yes, even I think this from time to time." A suggestion of a smile played on his lips. "You often hear of people keeling over and dying, don't you? Of natural causes. And then other people die suddenly, from some unnatural act of violence."

"What's an unnatural act of violence?"

"Well, I don't know. People who commit suicide use unnatural violence on themselves, don't they?"

"People who are murdered also die from unnatural violence."

"I wasn't thinking of murder, but now that you mention it, that's true, of course."

NOTE

Douglas Oliver, "The Three Lilies", in *Lamb*, 3, ed. Anthony Barnett (1982); extended repr. as "Three Lilies", in *Poets on Writing: Britain, 1970–1991*, ed. Denise Riley (Macmillan, 1982)

Natsume Sōseki, *Kokoro*, trans. Ewin McClellan (Tuttle, 1957)

Natsume Sōseki, *Kokoro*, trans. Meredith McKinney (Penguin, 2010)

Victor Segalen

It is time to sing the praises of Victor Segalen, in particular just now Timothy Billings and Christopher Bush's near faultless translation and presentation of *Stèles*, published in two volumes by Wesleyan University Press in 2007. I have already mentioned this tour de force in the opening gambit to my very first Antonym, "On a Translation", about Andrea Zanzotto. How did Segalen find his way, in passing, into a piece about Zanzotto? I was responding to a reviewer who thought that an earlier, certainly, in that respect, ground-breaking, version of a selection of *Stèles*, was to be preferred. Fortunately, that online review, which made startlingly embarrassing assertions, has disappeared.

I suppose that in certain respects Segalen as an intellectual European in China might be considered a counterpart to Lafcadio Hearn in Japan. But whereas one has the impression that all Japanese have heard of, with affection, Hearn, my mentioning Segalen to Chinese scholars of Western poetry has been met pretty much with blank stares, at most a vague recollection of a name but not the work. If by and large that really is the case, it is a loss. Nor do I think that that has happened because one, a Graeco-Irishman, professionally a journalist, later an academic, is writing in English and the other, professionally a naval doctor and an archaeologist, is writing in French. Anyway, Hearn was also a francophile, who translated French authors into English and spent ten years in New Orleans writing about, among other things, of course, French opera and Creole culture. Yet, this cannot be the whole story because some of Segalen's works are translated into Chinese, including *Stèles*, at least twice—*Bei* (Beijing, 1993), *Gu jin bei lu* [Segalen's Chinese, meaning "Transcriptions of Ancient and Modern Steles" or "A Record of Steles Old and New"] (Taipai, 1999). But it took that long, some eighty years, for a work written in and so to speak about China and indeed first printed there, privately in 1912, then, with extra poems, in 1914. Remarkably, there is a translation into Japanese of

[76]

Segalen's collected writings, with *Stèles* included in *Segaren chosakushū*, vol. 6 (Tokyo, 2002). Well, I shouldn't make too much of these things, especially as I am more than a little out of my depth. Nevertheless, in discussing nineteenth-century Chinese intellectuals, a great author and scholar could comment: "Yet as to Western literature, they all showed a stony incuriosity inexcusable even on the plea of their ignorance of the languages."—*A Collection of Qian Zhongshu's English Essays* (Beijing, 2005).

Stèles are not at all, despite the declaration in Segalen's Chinese title, transcriptions or translations of what is to be found written on actual steles. They are entirely original imaginative poems. They simply, or, rather, complexly, draw and adapt their material substance from historical, legendary, and invented, sources. In fact, Haun Saussy opens with a foreword entitled "*Impressions de Chine*, Or How to Translate from a Nonexistent Original", which sums things up very nicely.

It is possible to read *Stèles* with enormous pleasure, with frequent puzzlement, without the commentary provided by Billings and Bush. But the way this edition is presented is so relevant, so beautiful, an object lesson, that for once one does not decry the apparatus of translator explanation. A lengthy introduction by the translators prefaces facsimile pages of the first complete 1914 edition, published from France but printed in China, which face the translations. Copious notes and bibliographies end this vol. 1 print edition. Understandably, vol. 2 is a downloadable pdf, in which Segalen's Chinese sources and contexts are exhaustively investigated. It is not essential for a reading and appreciation of vol. 1 but it is fascinating, deeply informative, and recommended.

What of the translations themselves? They are, in my view, immaculate —almost: it's niggardly but I do wonder at the translation of Pei-king as Bei-jing in the poems—the title page shows Péking as the place of printing. Segalen's hyphen is kept but it wasn't known to us as Beijing at the time he wrote and the compromise looks odd. Otherwise, these translations are unafraid to find exact equivalence in structure, vocabulary, meaning and tone. They do not add. They do not subtract. They do not reduce what is there. They do not suggest what is not there. No false or gratuitous poeticisms or I-know-betters-than-the-original. I want to nail one thing on the head. The two earliest translations of *Stèles* title the first four sections "Stelae/Steles Facing South / North / East / West", while the third titles them "Steles Set South / North / East / West". These are correct interpretations for South and North—"Stèles face au Midi / Nord"—but they are not correct for East and West because Segalen writes "Stèles Orientées" and "Stèles Occidentées" in an absolutely crucial departure from what he could have written but did not: "Stèles face à l'Est / Ouest". Billings and Bush correctly translate "Oriented Stèles" and "Occidented Stèles". It is as well to point out that, with reason, they keep the French spelling *Stèles* for the book title and its poems while turning to steles when talking about the actual statuary.

I had thought to subject all four translations to comparative detective agency stuff but, honestly, there is little point. While the three earlier translations are serviceable, sometimes elegant, in their different ways none achieves the close to perfection of the Billings and Bush. By all means go to them and test this if you wish.

Segalen wrote in two stèles which he omitted from his book:

> The Master says:
>
> [...]
>
> Description encloses a gesture as a contour; traps
> color beneath an exact reflection; the word
> in the servile and measured echo. Practice
> Description; make only good use of it.
>
> [...]
>
> —
>
> I say:
>
> Description kills the gesture as frozen air kills
> breath. Dead is the color that reflects but
> does not illuminate. Refrain from descrip-
> tion and its handiwork.
>
> [...]

Translations of *Stèles*

Stelae, trans. Nathaniel Tarn (Santa Barbara, Unicorn, 1969), bilingual selection

"Steles", in Michael Anthony Taylor, "Victor Segalen: A Critical Edition of the Complete Verse in English Translation, with Notes and an Introduction", Ph.D. dissertation (Berkeley, University of California, 1978), available from Proquest Dissertations

Steles, trans. Michael Taylor (Santa Monica, Lapis, 1987)

Steles, trans. Andrew Harvey, & Iain Watson (London, Cape, 1990), omits the integral Chinese epigraphs, quite possibly a publisher decision

Stèles, trans. Timothy Billings, & Christopher Bush (Middletown, CT, Wesleyan University Press, 2007), bilingual, the only published translation that explains the Chinese epigraphs; two vols: vol. 1, *Stèles*, print; vol. 2, *Stèles: Chinese Sources and Contexts*, pdf

Other translated works by Segalen

René Leys, trans. Y. A. Underwood (Chicago, J. P. O'Hara, 1974; New York, Overlook, 1989; London, Quartet, 1990; New York, New York Review of Books, 2003), semi-autobiographical novel set in China

The Great Statuary of China, trans. Eleanor Levieux (Chicago, & London, University of Chicago Press, 1978), awkward trans., includes photos of a few steles

"Odes" and "Tibet", in Michael Anthony Taylor, ibid., Taylor established, with the assistance of Segalen's daughter, Annie Joly-Segalen, the first full text of *Thibet*, published by Mercure de France in 1979

A Lapse of Memory, trans. Rosemary Arnoux (Mount Nebo, Queensland, Boombana, 1995), novel about the loss of Tahitian culture after contact with Europeans

Paintings, trans. Andrew Harvey, & Iain Watson (London, Quartet, 1991), imaginative prose-poem essays on Chinese art

Essay on Exoticism: An Aesthetics of Diversity, trans. Yaël Rachel Schlick (Durham, & London, Duke University Press, 2002)

"Five Paintings", trans. Anthony Barnett, in *Snow lit rev*, 4 (spring 2016), not included by Segalen in *Peintures* (1916), first published posthumously 1981, not translated in *Paintings* (1991) or elsewhere

BECKETT AND JAZZALITY

THIS IS A NON-REVIEW of a new book about Samuel Beckett: *Beckett and Musicality* edited by Sara Jane Bailes and Nicholas Till (Ashgate, 2014). I can't review it because a review copy is not available and I shall neither buy it nor look for it in a library. I have glanced at the contents list, the index, and the editors' introduction, downloaded from the publisher website. I have minimally discussed it with a colleague who does have it. It is, I think, only the second book wholly devoted to Beckett and music. The first was Mary Bryden's *Samuel Beckett and Music* (OUP, 1998), in which one finds a passing reference to jazz. Bryden is a contributor to the new book. Like *Samuel Beckett and Music*, *Beckett and Musicality* is important for what it covers but from my perspective—and I hope not only mine—it is lacking in what it does not cover. Jazz is awfully absent.

Beckett and Musicality is the fruit of the *Beckett and Music Symposium* organized by the editors at the University of Sussex on 27 February 2009 under the umbrella of the Centre for Research in Opera and Music Theatre. The book includes additional contributions and omits one, in particular.

Disclosure. I was alerted to the approaching symposium, to be held just down the road from my house, by a colleague. After some hesitant toing and froing my suggestion that I contribute was accepted. In fact, I put my foot down with a firm hand, so to speak. Yes or No. Drawing on my book *Listening for Henry Crowder: A Monograph on His Almost Lost Music* (Allardyce Book, 2007), and its accompanying CD, I gave a presentation of pianist and vocalist Henry Crowder's 1930 settings of poems by Beckett and Nancy Cunard, who was Crowder's lover, entitled "Only Poet, Shining Whore", from the title of Beckett's poem "From the Only Poet to a Shining Whore *(For Henry Crowder to Sing.)*". What I had to say and play appeared to be appreciated by, in particular, the symposium's younger participants from abroad, but not only, and it may have opened a few ears. One noted specialist told me that now she had heard Crowder, and Yan Pevsner accompanying vocalist

Allan Harris in new recordings, play his music she understood how to approach what had previously defeated her pianistic reading efforts.

The time came to submit my proposal for *Beckett and Musicality*. It was found wanting. I was asked to rewrite it. I couldn't. Given the earlier toing and froing I felt sure that my unacademic, so viewed, approach, however rigorous in its own way, was never going to pass muster. I was not prepared to risk more lost energy. I withdrew, politely. Sighs of relief all round, I can imagine. Yet strict adherence to accepted academic protocol isn't always a good idea. In fact it's a shame. Things get lost. Here is my proposal, exactly but for the square-bracketed note, as sent to the editors in 2011:

"Only Poet, Shining Whore" was the title of my presentation of Henry Crowder's settings of poems by Beckett and Nancy Cunard, and others, given at the *Beckett and Music Symposium* at University of Sussex. The title refers to the poem "From the Only Poet to a Shining Whore" written by Beckett for Crowder to set to music in 1930.

My paper was taken up to quite an extent with the playing of recordings. While wishing to keep this presentation title, the paper I would like to write for the proposed Ashgate volume would extend this consideration to Beckett's relationship with jazz more generally, including some related matters about art songs, improvisation and the origins of so-called Poetry and Jazz—a moot subject.

It appears that few researchers are properly aware that Beckett had more than just a nodding acquaintance with jazz. In addition to his Paris friendship with Cunard's consort, pianist Henry Crowder (who, incidentally, helped Cunard print Beckett's first book *Whoroscope* at The Hours Press), Beckett translated significant French texts about jazz for Cunard's famous 1934 *Negro: An Anthology*. Talking off-session about this with some of the other participants at the symposium gave me to understand that this is often overlooked. In fact, at my mention of Louis Armstrong, a respected elder of Beckett studies looked at me blankly and said that Beckett wouldn't know anything about that, until I drew his attention to Beckett's translation of a poem entitled "Armstrong". [He was duly regaled with my mean impression of a satchelmouth vocal.] While Beckett's work for *Negro* was obviously a commissioned job, it nevertheless points to his knowledge. I do not want to suggest that Beckett was a whole-hearted lover of jazz—probably, for reasons I wish to investigate, he was not—and he later expressed, in my opinion unwarranted, reservations about his poem and Crowder's setting—but there is a story to be told about his involvement. Beckett's brother Frank, with whom he often played music of one kind or another, was an amateur jazz pianist.

My paper would draw substantially on my research for my 2007 book+CD *Listening for Henry Crowder: A Monograph on His Almost Lost Music* but would develop matters relating to Beckett, and poetry and jazz and related musics, beyond what I could go into in the book. Seán Lawlor, in reviewing the book in *The Beckett Circle / Le Cercle de Beckett: Newsletter of the Samuel Beckett Society* (Fall 2008), wrote "I cannot imagine anyone who has an interest in Beckett's poems or his development in the 1930s not enjoying this book." [www.abar.net/crowdereviews.htm]

I haven't looked that out in a very long time and I wondered whether I was going to see a piece of fluff. But no. I don't think so. There's nothing wrong with it. Expansiveness would have followed. It should have been accepted. Now that I no longer wish to devote much time to the subject it will have to become someone else's task but I do offer a few pointers.

As far as I am aware no one has really investigated Beckett's evidently intermittent but significant crossings with jazz outside my own *Listening for Henry Crowder* [there are updates at www.abar.net/crowder.htm] and the generalized documentation of his translations for Cunard's *Negro: An Anthology*, dedicated to Crowder, gathered in Alan Warren Friedman's *Beckett in Black and Red: The Translations for Nancy Cunard's Negro (1934)* (University of Kentucky Press, 2000, repr., 2014). There among some nineteen pieces are Beckett's translations of Ernst Moerman's poem "Armstrong" and two pioneering articles by Robert Goffin: "The Best Negro Jazz Orchestras", substantially about Duke Ellington*, and "Hot Jazz". Tangential items include Bejamin Péret "Black and White in Brazil", George Sadoul "Sambo without Tears", and René Crevel "The Negress in the Brothel".

Beckett's cousin Sheila Page reminisces on Frank Beckett's jazz piano playing and Sam's Schubert, "I remember them playing duets", in James Knowlson's *Beckett Remembering Remembering Beckett* (Bloomsbury, 2006).

---

*Reinhold Wagnleiter, *Coca-Colonization and the Cold War: The Cultural Mission of the United States in Austria after the Second World War*, trans. Diana M Wolf (University of North Carolina Press, 1994, repr., 2007), writes: "Samuel Beckett's first published work was a review of Duke Ellington's music." This is an understandable but mistaken reference to Beckett's translation, however creative, of Robert Goffin's "The Best Negro Jazz Orchestras", not that that was by any means Beckett's first published item. The citation has currency so it is as well to point it out.

Mary Bryden notes about *Endgame* that Lawrence Shainberg "could relate the play's quips and responses in performance to the lightness and mutability of jazz, so that the exchanges between Nagg and Nell could be described thus: 'Each was a measure, clearly defined, like a jazz riff, subordinated to the rhythm of the whole.'"

In *Samuel Beckett's Waiting for Godot* (Chelsea House, 1988), Harold Bloom vividly relates director Herbert Blau's apprehension before a performance at San Quentin in 1957—the first play performed at the penitentiary since Sarah Bernhardt appeared there in 1913. Blau addressed the audience beforehand and "compared the play to a piece of jazz music 'to which one must listen for whatever one may find in it'." Correspondence reveals that in 1959 director Alan Schneider and Grove Press publisher Barney Rosset suggested to Beckett that *Krapp's Last Tape* might be performed at New York's "rather well-known bohemian cabaret", The Five Spot, home, for example, to Thelonious Monk and, now and then, poetry readings, but the idea of such a smoky and talkative atmosphere did not find favour.

I shall close with a Beckett quote from Tom F. Driver's "Beckett by the Madeleine", *Columbia University Forum*, vol. 4 (1961), a now famous interview cited by Maria Ristani in "Articulate Arrythmia: Samuel Beckett's Shorter Plays" in *Beckett and Musicality*. The quote I want reads, "What I am saying does not mean that there will henceforth be no form in art. It only means that there will be new form, and that this form will be of a type that it admits the chaos and does not try to say that the chaos is really something else. The form and the chaos remain separate. The latter is not reduced to the former. That is why the form itself becomes a preoccupation, because it exists as a problem separate from the material it accomodates. To find a form that accomodates the mess, that is the task of the artist now."

Make of it what you will. Musically, I think I know what I make of it and that means talking about jazz and improvisation, as well as chance, which is a very different thing, and composition, including Derek Bailey's posthumously premiered, 21 November 2015, *No. 22: Ping*.

e detti
MDCCCXIX

L' Infinito

Idillio I

Sempre caro mi fu quest'ermo colle,
E questa siepe, che da tanta parte
De l'ultimo orizzonte il guardo esclude.
Ma sedendo e mirando, interminato
Spazio di là da quella, e sovrumani
Silenzi, e profondissima quiete
Io nel pensier mi fingo, ove per poco
Il cor non si spaura. E come il vento
Odo stormir tra queste piante, io quello
Infinito silenzio a questa voce
Vo comparando: e mi sovvien l'eterno,
E le morte stagioni, e la presente
E viva, e 'l suon di lei. Così tra questa
Infinità
Immensità s'annega il pensier mio:
E 'l naufragar m'è dolce in questo mare.

Leopardi, L'Infinito, 1819, note the capitalized L'I in the manuscripts. In line 14 Leopardi first
wrote Immensità which he cancelled for Infinità before evidently restoring Immensità in print

LEOPARDI AND THE INFINITE

OVER ALMOST TWO HUNDRED YEARS since Leopardi wrote his poem, "L'Infinito" has been translated countless times into many languages, of which at least a dozen or so are in English, not counting a number of exegeses. Why try again? Forgetting the odd clanger and howler, they all have faults of vocabulary or structure, some weirdly contorted, some serious, others less so, which is not to say that mine is perfect because it is not. For example, in lines 2–3, unhappy with the English "which" it should be, I first chose, for what I thought was resonance and fluency, "This hedgerow too, although it closes off / From view a great deal of the far horizon." but a correspondent has alerted me to its negativity where Leopardi is positive. The hedge is dear to him not despite but rather because it closes off the view. After many trials I have, for the moment, if apprehensively, given "density" to the hedge, while restoring the phrasal order of the Italian:

> I have always loved this hill on its own,
> This hedgerow too, whose density a great deal
> Of the far horizon closes off from view.
> But sitting here reflecting, unending
> Spaces beyond all that, suprahuman
> Silences, and deep concerted stillness
> I picture in my mind's eye; until almost
> My heart has taken fright. And as the breeze
> I listen to rustles in these leaves, to such
> Infinite silence I begin to compare
> This song: and I summon the eternal,
> And the dead seasons, and the present
> And living, and the sound of its voice. So
> In this immensity my mind goes under:
> And my foundering at sea is sweet.

I want to home in on two words: *ermo* in the first line and *dolce* in line 15, which is the last line. They are tips of the iceberg, so to speak.

It is, I am sure, quite wrong to translate *ermo* as *lonely*, which is what the majority of translators and commentators do. The hill, the object, the subject, in Leopardi's sight, identified as Monte Tabor, little more than a stone's throw beyond Recanati, even if, even though, Leopardi has pushed it off into his imagination, is not so much *lonely* as perhaps *solitary*, which a couple of translators do turn to. Rare *ermo*, from the Greek, has no happy equivalence in English. Naturally, one thinks of *remote*, but the hill is not really that either, nor is our English word so rare. Recognizing the difficulties, three translators go for *hermit's, secluded, lonesome*. My *on its own* is commonplace yet, rather like Lowell's elaborate *pushed off by itself*, which reveals a sentient truth, might be thought unexpected and, in that sense, rare. It seeks its own difference. Stretching it a bit I dare say. In French, Bonnefoy gives *colline solitaire* and Estève *coteau solitaire*, while Jaccottet gives *hauteur déserte*. As we see, they cannot agree the translation of *colle*. All the English translations I have read have hill. Might one opt for *col* as a translation of *colle* into English, thereby transferring rarity to the hill itself? If only, but, like *ermo* and *remote*, they are false friends. Yet in *Zibaldone: The Notebooks of Leopardi* (Farrar, Straus and Giroux; & Penguin, 2013) we read: "Regarding the sensations that please on account of indefiniteness alone, see my idyll on the *infinite*, and recall the idea of a steeply sloping countryside where the view at a certain distance does not reach as far as the valley, and that of a row of trees, whose end is lost from sight, either because of the length of the row, or because it is situated in the dip, etc. etc. etc."—from Z 1430–1431 (1 August 1821). I don't think this is satisfactorily solved and I am sure there is more work to be done.

At first, I sought to avoid translating *dolce* as *sweet*. However correct, I thought there had to be a better word in English than this seemingly weak one, for all sorts of sugary reasons. But no, *sweet* is absolutely essential. It must be appreciated that *acqua dolce* means *fresh water*, an English synonym of which is *sweet water*. So in considering the last word *mare, sea*, which is *salt water, dolce* takes on a contradictory significance in which sinking in this sea, or *going under* as I have it, whether or not actually drowning, is not after all a salty thing but a restorative, refreshing, sweet thing.

In support of my argument, if such is needed, for I found this after my translation was done, I quote from a letter to Pietro Giordani dated 30 April 1817—"L'Infinito" is two years later—in which Leopardi writes of Recanati, inland but no more than ten kilometres as the crow flies from what was then its coastal fishing port, now a resort: "You have been misinformed that the air of this city is salubrious. It is very changeable, damp, salty, hard on the nerves and no good at all for certain constitutions on account of its thinness."—*The Letters of Giacomo Leopardi, 1817–1837*, selected and trans. Prue Shaw (Leeds, Northern Universities, 1998). It is my understanding that what I take to be a conscious antimony has passed unnoticed in Leopardi studies, whether in English, Italian, or elsewhere.

The two most recent translations with the widest currency, by Galassi and Parks, are no less troublesome than others. Why? after so many years is a rhetorical question. In keeping with another translator, Galassi starts off on a wrong foot by deciding that the title means "Infinity". It does not. But then how much good can be said of Galassi's *Canti* (Penguin, 2010; FSG, 2012) all round. It attends to neither accuracy nor the imaginative. It is all over the place. That the complete task he set himself is heroic cannot be an excuse. Both Galassi, and Parks in a translation embedded in his introduction to *Passions* (Yale–Margellos, 2014), a rather differently-voiced selected translation than the committee-translated complete *Z*, about which he was backhanded in *NYRB*, are stuck on *lonely*. Many see Leopardi as a lonely figure but whether he was or was not does not make a hill. Leopardi spoke of himself as *solitary*. Galassi, like almost all translators, gives the easy-to-settle-for and, as we have seen, all-important *sweet*.

Parks is unspeakable: *I find pleasure drowning*. True, Leopardi talks a great deal about pleasure in *Z* but that's not the poem. Two other translators are also all at sea with *pleasant* and *easeful*, while for a third, the most recent of all, it's, What? *a joy*. Unattributed poetry subtitles to *Il Giovane Favoloso*, a compassionate 2014 biopic, are, predictably, Galassi's.

Let the last word be Leopardi's. "Besides, sometimes the soul might desire, and actually does desire, a view that is restricted or confined in some way, as in Romantic situations. The reason is the same, a desire for the infinite, because then, instead of sight, the imagination is at work and the fantastic takes over from the real. The soul imagines what it cannot see, whatever is hidden by that tree, that hedge, that tower, and wanders in an imaginary space and pictures things in a way that would be impossible if its view could extend in all directions, because the real would exclude the imaginary."—from *Z* 171 (12–23 July 1820).

Not the last word. At last I find a place for this by Italo Calvino: "I find it very plausible that one can make the equivalent of a poem with the way one arranges trees, but I suspect that real trees are of little or no use for writing a poem about trees." and "Or that it makes no sense to expect a landscape to dictate poems to you, because a poem is made of ideas and words and syllables, whereas a landscape is composed of leaves and colours and light."—"Japan", in *Collection of Sand*, trans. M. L. McLaughlin (Penguin, 2013). Serendipitously, Xavier Kalck points to a Leopardian evocation in Louis MacNeice: "As with the hawthorn hedge, what lies beyond once more combines escape and the inescapable, 'infinite possibility' and 'a sense of eternity.'"—*Muted Strings: Louis MacNeice's* The Burning Perch (Paris, PUF–CNED, 2015). And then what is more: "From far away, peering gently and discreetly over at what is near at hand, we perceive something we would dearly love to have nearby: the unknown and yet all too intimate, familiar distance."—Robert Walser, "Watteau", in *Looking at Pictures*, trans. Susan Bernofsky (Christine Burgin / New Directions, 2015).

A Door Open to the Outside and to the Inside

In written in the margins of life Qian Zhongshu says why he prefers "Windows" to doors. At least that is how I read it—*Humans, Beasts and Ghosts: Stories and Essays*, ed. Christopher G. Rea (Columbia University, 2011): "Every room in the world has a door, but some rooms are without windows. This indicates that windows represent a higher stage of human evolution than doors. For a room's inhabitant a door is a necessity, whereas a window is to some extent a luxury."

"In novels, for instance, we read about thieves and lovers making clandestine rendezvous—both are fond of climbing through windows" and "he who enters through the front door is the son-in-law in name only, because even if the father-in-law approves of him he has yet to capture the heart of the young lady herself. It is those who enter through the back window who are the true lovers to whom maidens surrender themselves body and soul."

This is not unlike the restricted view through a window or the one expressed at the end of the Antonym "Leopardi and The Infinite", just before this one.

For some unfathomable reason I have lost my train of thought, it's been creeping up on me, and now I've forgotten the other bits and pieces I had in mind to quote.

I do not like doors, doors to cupboards or to the outside and so to the inside too. I do not want socks and pocket handkerchiefs and shirts and pants and all the rest hidden away in closed drawers and wardrobes.

Oh yes, in "On Writers" Qian reminds us that Théophile Gautier in *Les Grotesques* has this to say about the sickness known as *poésophobie*: "The story goes that a man of wealth one day happened to open his son's desk drawer, there espying a sheaf of writing paper covered with words. These papers were neither account registers nor debt ledgers—and while the first letter in each line was capitalized, the last letter for some reason stopped short of the right margin. After careful investigation, the father discovered that these papers were manuscripts of poetry. His heart seethed with fury, and he proceeded to fly into a rage." Lamenting the ill fortune that has befallen his family, insanity ensues. In my own words, what indeed is a father to do should he discover on opening a drawer that he has given birth not to an accomplished businessman but to a poet, of obscurity.

I want to leave the doors to the house open when the weather allows and I am in the house or when I am not in the house at least the back door. Or when the weather does not allow at least to leave it unlocked.

I shall not comment beyond this on the lecturer who would tell his students that a novelist who has a character going in and out the back door has a particular-part-of-the-anatomy fixation. Just now I am thinking of all those poor, unless they be wealthy, maidens who receive their lovers through the back window.

Nevertheless, the window is also a means to escape, in fairy tales of old or the bitter proposition of Isak Dinesen's *The Angelic Avengers*: "She was not certain either if, by herself, she would be able to open the heavy lock of the entrance door.

"She would have to find another way out. Outside her window was a balcony, and an old ivy twined its strong stems all the way from the ground to the balustrade. She had, before now, playfully pictured to herself how, by these, as by the steps of a ladder, Romeo might climb to her room. She did not know of giddiness, and she had no other way out."

Henry Crowder's Letters to Nancy Cunard

We try to fit the pieces together but sometimes there are too many
pieces or there are missing pieces or they might be the wrong shape

IN 2007 I PUBLISHED MY RESEARCH ON THE AFRICAN AMERICAN
pianist who was the consort of Nancy Cunard for some seven years from
1928, *Listening for Henry Crowder: A Monograph on His Almost Lost Music*. At the
time, I had sight of two letters written by Crowder deposited in the Cunard
collection at the Harry Ransom Research Center, University of Texas at
Austin: one dated 3 March 1934, congratulating her on the publication of
Negro: An Anthology, dedicated to Crowder; the other dated 11 August 1954,
thanking her for sending a copy of *Grand Man: Memories of Norman Douglas*,
published that year. I reproduced a brief holograph extract from each of
the letters.

On page 42 I discussed what purported to be two further letters written by Crowder to Cunard, both partly concerning Ezra Pound. One
dated, as we shall see ostensibly, 1952, cited in J. J. Wilhelm, *Ezra Pound:
The Tragic Years, 1925–1972* (1994); the other dated 1953, quoted by Anne
Chisholm in *Nancy Cunard: A Biography* (1979). In fact, Chisholm quoted
from two letters to which she had been given access, the other, not about
Pound, dated November 1954, the 29th as it turns out. In a footnote I
asked why the apparent owner of at least two letters would not reveal
himself or confirm their content, in particular in respect of Pound.

In June 2015, a collection of letters from Crowder to Cunard, laid into
a luxurious modernistic artist-designed album, was the major part of a lot,
one of many, sold at auction by Christie's at the realized price of £6,500 to
publisher and book dealer David Deiss, from the estate of book collector,
authority on Renaissance bindings, and himself an auctioneer, Anthony
Hobson, who died aged ninety-two in 2014. A copy of *Negro* was one of
the other lots. Hobson was Cunard's literary executor and negotiated the
sale of some of her papers now at Texas. But about half the Texas Cunard

holdings were acquired not from Hobson but from New York book dealer and auctioneer House of El Dieff, no longer in existence. The Texas holdings were the result of a series of purchases between 1969 and 1977. Cunard died in 1965 and Crowder in 1955. Texas is unsure but thinks that their two 1934 and 1954 letters may have been acquired from El Dieff in 1970. How those two letters in particular came to be separated from the rest is an open question but it can be noted that both have a point in common in that they were written in response to receiving books. In light of the album it does seem unreasonable to imagine that Hobson was the one who separated them. Perhaps it was Cunard herself.

I have been able to examine the contents of the tooled-leather album, quite a fetishistic object, commissioned by Hobson from P. L. Martin in 1971. It holds nine letters with five associated envelopes, two notes, two telegrams, three picture postcards with associated envelope, dated 1928 through 1934, and 1953, 1954, the latter two the letters from which Chisholm was able to quote. The earlier letters are mostly passionate declarations of love and longing. The lot also included a few photos of Crowder, Cunard, and both together, none previously unknown.

To return to Wilhelm's 1952 citation: such a letter from Crowder to Cunard cannot exist. Curiously, or significantly, Wilhelm does not include any Crowder letter in his list of correspondence locations. Wilhelm was too ill to talk with by the time I was able to make contact with his daughter while writing my book. His citation, again, significantly, not in quote marks, that Crowder thought Pound crazy as a fox is not to be found in any known Crowder letter. It does not occur in Crowder's description of Pound in the 1953 letter quoted by Chisholm. The wording of that letter makes clear that Crowder and Cunard had not been in contact for "so, so many years". Crowder does goes on to say that he was given a Paris address for Cunard by a fellow pianist but "This was some years ago, and I think I wrote to you, but I am not at all sure."

What, then, is to be made of Wilhelm's 1952 citation? It is certain that Crowder visited Pound at St Elizabeths at least during the latter half of the 1940s. Charles Olson wrote about an occasion when they happened to visit Pound at the same time. I had thought that this could be dated either in the first half of 1946 or on 9 February 1948 but, reviewing the evidence, including the content of 1946 correspondence between Cunard and Pound, it cannot be 1946. It appears that Cunard, after their final mid-1930s break-up, learned of Crowder's post-war whereabouts in 1947. In my book I discuss the circumstances surrounding that period and whether they may have been in touch, which remains very much an open question.

The conclusion seems to be that if Wilhelm had sight of a "crazy as a fox" letter, or was informed of one, his 1952 dating has to be wildly wrong. Much more likely, he has colourfully paraphrased Chisholm's 1953 quotation: "I have a sneaking suspicion that Ezra is putting on an act, and that he is saner than most people." Not, then, the more usual wily as a fox, but crazy as one.

To put it mildly, I am sorry that Hobson's Crowder letters were not available for examination while I was working on my book. They may not have added that much that was terribly important or strictly factual, or not already to be surmised, but to have had some dates and places, including the serendipitous confirmation of a theatre tour, and expressions of passionate or tender affection, with some tiffs, laid bare, would not have gone amiss.

In the posthumously published *As Wonderful As All That? Henry Crowder's Memoir of His Affair with Nancy Cunard, 1928–1935* (1987), Crowder says that in England "I had gotten around the permit question and had secured a fairly decent job in a theatre orchestra." I had surmised a date of 1933 or 1934 and a Buddy Bradley connection, the African American choreographer resident in London with whose brother, Arthur Bradley, Crowder appeared in Paris in 1936. With the Hobson album's three postcards mailed to Cunard in an envelope, postmarked 17 Oct 1934, Dudley, Worcs, in which Crowder writes that he will not be granted a work permit, the matter can now be laid to rest. Crowder's theatre engagement turns out to have been Sam Manning's *The Harlem Night-Birds*, with a black, mainly

"British", cast of some thirty-five, which played Dudley Opera House, destroyed in a fire in 1936, for a week from 15 October 1934, two days before Crowder's mailing. The revue opened at Queen's Theatre, Poplar, East London on 24 September, transferring to the Empress Theatre, Brixton, South East London for the week of 1 October, before touring England, Glasgow and Dublin through to the end of May 1935. Birmingham was the first stop before Dudley, and London again immediately after. It is quite on the cards that the dancer Adelaide Willoughly, with whom Crowder had become involved, and with whom he was to tour the Continent in a double act, was one of the show's "12 Dusky Harlem Girls". How long Crowder remained with the show is not known but he was certainly back in France by around spring 1935, in Cambrai, where he and Cunard parted company for good. Trinidadian orchestra leader and comedian Sam Manning, the consort of Amy Ashwood Garvey, estranged first wife of Marcus Garvey, served with the British West Indies Regiment during World War 1, entertaining troops in Palestine and Egypt. He moved to London from New York in 1934, returning there in 1941. Thus, three postcards in an envelope reveal the most interesting new fact to be found in all the correspondence.

I take the opportunity to list Hobson's Crowder letters here, with the barest detail, because I am in the fortunate position to be able to do so, but I am not free to transcribe them. In all likelihood the album may eventually be sold on to a research library or enter a new prolonged period of hibernation, away from inquisitive eyes, in another private collection. For the sake of completeness the two letters deposited with Texas are included in italic. Cunard's letters to Crowder are almost certainly not extant. Places, but not detailed addresses, are shown where known. Everything is handwritten, in ink, with a couple of pencil exceptions.

On learning of Crowder's death, Cunard wrote Charles Burkhart on 24 April 1955: "Henry made me—and so be it." (

Friday afternoon, postmark 21.9.28, Venice to Florence
letter and envelope incl. expressions of love, water damaged

Sunday, postmark 24.IX.28, Venice to Florence
letter and envelope incl. expressions of love

Tuesday, 3 P.M., not stamped, prob. delivered by hand, Venice to Venice
letter and envelope, apology for lapse of behaviour in reply to a letter
from Cunard

Thursday, postmark 26.X.1928, Paris to London
letter and envelope incl. expressions of love

12.07, 27 Oc 28, Paris to London
telegram, confirming letters received and sent

Sunday morning, 8.45, date unknown, location unknown
letter incl. expressions of love, water damaged

date unknown, location uncertain, poss. Chapelle Réanville
brief note

date unknown, location uncertain, poss. Chapelle Réanville
brief regretful note

date unknown, Paris to Chapelle Réanville
telegram incl. tells of brilliant opening with Victor present, i.e., Nancy's
cousin Victor Cunard

Sunday eve, 18.30, date unknown, location uncertain, prob. Chapelle
Réanville
letter incl. expressions of love

Monday Night, 10:0, location uncertain, prob. Chapelle Réanville
incl. expressions of love and talk of Anna, prob. Nancy's housekeeper

Saturday March 3, 34, prob. London to London
letter in which Crowder writes about Negro: An Anthology

postmark 17 Oct 1934, Dudley, Worcs. to London
three picture postcards of Dudley, with envelope, on which Crowder
writes that he has received a letter from his solicitor saying he will not be
granted a permit to work in England, that he has overstayed his visit, that
unless his manager can adjust this he will have to return to France, that
he will see Nancy on Sunday

Oct. 27 - 1953, Washington D.C. to Paris
letter and envelope incl. about Ezra Pound and Norman Douglas

8 - 11 - 1954 [11 August], Washington D.C. to London
letter in which Crowder writes about Grand Man: Memories of Norman Douglas

11 - 29 - 54
Washington D.C. to poss. Lamothe-Fénelon
letter incl. about Washington, Marion Anderson, Norman Douglas

———

Henry Crowder, with Hugo Speck, *As Wonderful As All That? Henry Crowder's Memoir
of His Affair with Nancy Cunard, 1928–1935* (Navarro, CA, Wild Trees Press, 1987)
Anthony Barnett, *Listening for Henry Crowder: A Monograph on His Almost Lost Music*
(Lewes, E. Suss., Allardyce Book, 2007), incl. extensive bibliography and CD
updated at www.abar.net/crowder.htm
With grateful thanks to David Deiss, Christie's, Harry Ransom Research Center
Anne Chisholm, John Cowley, Konrad Nowakowski, Howard Rye, Val Wilmer

NANCY and HENRY
album designed by P L Martin, 1971
black, white, silver, two shades of grey, double C motif on both covers
courtesy David Deiss, photo Christie's

Eileen Chang and Isak Dinesen

In june 2015 I took the unusual step, for me, of dashing off a squib to *The Times* in response to an item about famous authors who had successfully mastered a second language in which to write, their original works or their own translations or, rather, new writings, of their works. Kundera, Nabokov, Beckett, Conrad were named. In other words, the usual suspects. Not a woman in sight. Where is the great Eileen Chang? I wrote, Where is the great Isak Dinesen? Of course—I am not sure why "of course"—my letter was not published.

It so happens that I was in the middle of reading Chang's *Naked Earth* (1956), in Chang's translation—she wrote some other works directly in English—reissued in 2015 more or less at the same time as the publication of *The Festival of Insignificance*, the translation of Kundera's *La fête de l'insignifiance* (2014), which he wrote in French. It was that book that prompted the *Times* piece.

Doubtless, Eileen Chang (1920–1995) is best known in the West as the author of the novella "Lust, Caution", written in Chinese, begun in the early 1950s, published 1979, filmed 2007, the same year in which an English translation, by Julia Lovell, first appeared. At least, the film is well-known, if not always the author whose work it is based: "What are you reading?" "*Naked Earth*. Quite tragic. Set in the early days of Mao. By Eileen Chang." "Oh?" "She wrote the story "Lust, Caution", made into that film." "Ah!"

I didn't like the film. In "Lust, Caution" the erotic relationship is understated, discreet. Only the title truly betrays the unsaid. Not so in *Lust, Caution*, which is indiscreet, explicit. Scenes were cut in the version released in some countries, notably, mainland China, perhaps in this case for the good. It is not that Chang does not write openly about sex. She does that in *Naked Earth*, which is a story of love, close to flowering, between two young people ruined by others in positions of, or with access to, authority. Even through the brutality, though, Chang can write, "She stared at the glass of tea on his desk. Imprisoned under the glass lid a white jasmine was drifting very slowly down through the yellowish green twilight of the tea and another flower was rising, both with the utter purposelessness and unconcern of clouds." Beautiful in its foreboding.

Isak Dinesen aka Karen Blixen (1885–1962) is another great author probably best known now because of a film. In her case, her autobiographical *Out of Africa*, with Meryl Streep in the title role. But, I implore you, do not confuse Blixen–Dinesen with Streep. Rather, think of her as the author of, for example, the novellas "Babette's Feast", which, when it was turned into a film in 1987, had its location, I suppose for logistic reasons, transported from the coast of Norway to the coast of Denmark; and "The Immortal Story", filmed in 1968 by Orson Welles as *Une histoire immortelle*, with Jeanne Moreau, originally for French television, set in nineteenth-century Macau, though Dinesen's novella takes place in what is now Guangzhou, at the time Canton. These are magic films. Both novellas are collected in Dinesen's *Anecdotes of Destiny* (1958), which she wrote, like most of her work, in English.

Two great and miraculous writers. And, as I see, that China connection. Now for something else:

> "'I am unhappy, Father," I said. "I have loved this town and the people in it. I have drunk them down with delight. But they have some poison in them which I cannot stand. If I think of them now, I vomit up my soul. Do you know a cure for me?"
>
> "'Why yes," he said, "I know a cure for everything: salt water."
>
> "'Salt water?" I asked him.
>
> "'Yes," he said, "in one way or the other. Sweat, or tears, or the salt sea."
>
> 'I said: "I have tried sweat and tears. The salt sea I meant to try, but a woman in black lace prevented me."

So wrote Isak Dinesen in "The Deluge at Norderney" in *Seven Gothic Tales* (1934). Welles planned to film this for TV too, as a twofer, but it never got off the ground. Nor did he finish a later attempt, along with "The Dreamers", another of the *Tales*.

DIBDABS

HE LIKED TO SAY he was as old as the hills but not as old as the mountains. When a young woman was curious enough to ask how old he was he misheard and gave out the year of his birth. In this way he was always 41. Then always they both would laugh.

✻

THE GRASS HAS BEEN MOWN on the path that winds alongside the brook. It makes it easier to walk and avoid the nettles on either side but somehow I wish they'd left it overgrown.

Within spitting distance, imaginatively speaking, on the other side of the river proper, a luxury riverside development of houses is under construction. The one long slender crane, motionless at about a 45° angle, reminds me of a long range gun, immense range more like it. Luxury? Relatively speaking, otherwise it sounds most doubtful. Three pigeons are drawing near to my feet. I'm sitting on a semi-circular wide-depth backless wooden plank bench. They are pecking at grass seed it seems, not particularly paying attention to anything or anyone else. A fourth pigeon has arrived and now they are moving away in concert, still pecking. Ever since I learnt that the figure four is inauspicious because in Japanese the kanji for four sounds exactly the same as the kanji for death—it's like that in Chinese—I have, I have to admit, been superstitious (now there are just three again) and I try to avoid fours of things, like sweets or tomatoes on a plate. It doesn't work with things like chair legs or the wheels on a car (one doesn't usually even get a spare narrow-profile fifth in the boot anymore, only a temporary repair kit you hope you will never have to fiddle with). Then @y@ says to me it's sometimes good to eat up death. You don't have to tell me, completely daft. Now there are five. The fifth is cooing and courting. Fickle. He doesn't care which one. He's flown away now, off and away across the river. It's strange what your eyes alight on if you take a moment's pause. A dead bicycle chain snaking in the grass by my right foot. The following day it's gone.

*

I NEED YOU, I really do need you, I really do need you to write, to live wouldn't be bad either. But you don't need to know this. Only I need to know this.

I read to escape, no, no, that should read need to escape from bad influences. Influences that try to tell me I should be writing this way (not actually *this* way right now) and that way. The resistance has to be strong. I can't (I don't mean don't) care if you don't like it. I may not know what I am doing but I know it better than you.

A vacancy. There is a vacancy.

I'm not saying that's what I agree with.

*

STOP SMOKING I want to say to the young girls. I don't care about the boys. Stop using your cell phones while you are pushing your pushchairs almost as if into oblivion on these pavements, which might be narrow or might be crowded, I want to say to the young mothers. Usually I don't. When I was just a little boy I do remember my excitement at seeing a cartoon on children's television in which the cars drove on the pavement, directionally on each side, and the people walked in the road. I can't remember if that was directional in lanes or a jumble, or how they got to the shops. I'd like to see it again but I haven't been able to find it. I don't think I imagined it. It was black and white, then again that might have been because television wasn't in colour then.

❧

European Misery

I READ FROM A PUBLISHER of my acquaintance, I must make clear not the publisher of my pasquinade "The Publisher", that exquisite suffering is supposed to be, in the sense that it seems to be not that it should be, the default mode of the beautifully written short story, or the portrait, daubs or photographs. To which I rejoin that it is also the marked characteristic of the particular kind of beautifully written Central and East European novel beautifully translated into English. Heaven knows the not so distant past deserves all that. Erpenbeck. I'm sorry. I cannot read this. I try. In fact I do. But I wish I hadn't. Epigraph from Sebald. We've had a surfeit of it. Kertész. All right.

European Boredom

KUNDERA'S THE FESTIVAL OF INSIGNIFICANCE. So what. Opening on the length of the thigh, the buttock, the breast, each now supplanted by the young girls' navel. But he's missed a trick or two. The nape of the neck and there's nothing amiss with the shorter thigh.

CÉSAR VALLEJO'S POETRY, all of it, is well known in the English speaking world, in quite a few translations, some good, some indifferent. With a few exceptions, such as the novel *Tungsten*, little of his substantial other writing has been available. So *Selected Writings of César Vallejo*, trans., with others, and ed., Joseph Mulligan (Wesleyan University Press, 2015) should be a cause for celebration. But it isn't exactly that. Its structure is badly flawed, in contrast, for example, to the same publisher's magnificent handling of Victor Segalen's *Stèles*. It has to be said that it is not infrequent for seemingly all-embracing selected volumes to make for inadequate reading. *The Selected Poetry and Prose of Andrea Zanzotto* is another case in point. Without extreme rigour selections seem cursed. This is not to say that one should not read this Vallejo. One really should because some eighty percent of its content has never been translated into English before. Unfortunately, the wonderful wealth of very well translated prose, extracted from the great deal more that exists: university thesis, articles, chronicles, fiction, theatre, letters—almost everything is prefixed with a "From"—has, interspersed among it, selections from Vallejo's poetry, the majority in previously published, easily available translation from California's *The Complete Poetry* (2007), all anyway translated before by someone or other, more than once. What is more, the whole is divided into five notional "Books", representing different periods. Thus, work in any one genre is dispersed throughout these "Books". All this makes for irritating intrusion on the one hand and confusion on the other, not the helpful context the editor and publisher presumably intended. The encumbrance of the albatross. And that space taken up with poems could have been used for more of the wished for prose. Mulligan himself, in his introduction, identifies an urgent need for the publication of seven discrete volumes of the various works.

A few other carps. Firstly, the earliest Vallejo prose, taken from his thesis, includes short quotations from poems by two other poets, which are not translated. But this book is offered as a translation. Doubtless many of its readers will be unable to read Spanish well or at all. So why is it assumed that translations of those quotations are not wanted, alongside the originals? Secondly, Mulligan's fast-paced introduction—rather too full of contractions for my taste—makes for a concise, precise, introduction to Vallejo's life and work. What a shame, then, that near the end he has to invoke those ridiculous L=A=N=G=U=A=G=E poets and critics, a smarter set of scoundrels as one could ever hope not to meet. Mulligan might have taken a leaf out of his translation of Vallejo's article "Against Professional Secrets"—then again perhaps not because he published his translation of *Against Professional Secrets*, a different, posthumous, work, with the Roof home-L=A=N=D: "Abril could've tangled up the syntax and logic to join those masses of quacks who, with this or that avant-garde label, completely infest the environment." A bit rich coming from Vallejo, looking at his own poetic practice? Not at all. There is always reason to Vallejo's rebellious rhyme. Thirdly, that part of the bibliography, described as selected, devoted to "Works by Vallejo in English Translation", is nevertheless grossly negligent, and I don't think by accident, with significant omissions, notably Shearsman's *The Complete Poems* (2012), and quite a few others, including ABP's *The Black Heralds* (1995). That the Shearsman volume is print on demand can hardly be the reason for that, at least, not an acceptable one. Heaven knows, university presses themselves now resort to POD, in their cases in, more often than not without point-of-sale disclosure, shabby, shoddily printed enterprises—Columbia, New York, Oxford, Princeton among them; at least the Wesleyan is not that. No longer print no demand.

"Who flies further? Who throws better punches? Come on, who? Who breaks the record in tennis, in football, in duration, in altitude, in weight, in resistance, in intensity? Who earns more money? Who's the fastest dancer? The record for fasting, smoking, philately; the record for music, laughter, piety, matrimony, divorce, murder, revolution! . . ."—"Life as a Match". To which I reply, Who else writes like that? Where have I read such literary tumbling before, and that conversation, engaged in with the reader? Oh, yes, Mandelstam. Vallejo's prose: it's—yes, a contraction, they're not always bad—mostly wonderful, wonderfully translated—that pesky over-indulgence in unsuitable contractions aside—and that, I suppose, is what should count. Vallejo's Parisian reports for the Peruvian press are one with Osip Mandelstam and Joseph Roth. They have that same observed contradiction, wry, sardonic, ironic immediacy and interest, not without generosity either, and a natural, or it is hard-won, grace rarely found among the dross contributed by our clever personality intellectuals to the Anglo press. "Behold this ambiguous hypogeum, its iridescent paneling, a boisterous alveolus of cosmopolitan mange. Behold the loud café, armed with artists, with slackers, with snobs and wavering skirts, between Mimi and Margarita, between *grisette* and *garçonne*."—"La Rotonde". Vallejo is with Musil and Roth, rather than Mandelstam, in sceptical enthusiasm for the cinema: "In Paris rhetoric still receives applause ["stills" a typo?]. For *Chantecler*, Edmond Rostand still gets a twenty-year-old ovation, and the crowing of the rooster in his story still moistens the eyes of fiancées with the usual tears. When Victor Francen, of Theater Saint-Martin, with his luxurious dark orange plumage and his valiant cardboard crest, climbs atop the hedges and crows, 'Cock-a-doodle-doo! Cock-a-doodle-doo!' the balconies still creak, and the audience responds with grand syncopated applause."—"Contribution to Film Studies". These at random. Could I choose better? "In these disputes over film, only the profane are authorized to opine."—"Avant-garde Religions". "Solidarity? Cooperation? The cooperation of chancellors, the protocol of conveniences frequent and always to the advantage of Europe. Cooperation? Soon enough we shall demand it of them by way of the fist. In the meantime, let's breed a *ferpery*, a brood of Firpo, and Carpentier, soon you shall see. / Down with the empire. Here we are, the barbarians."—"Cooperation". Enough. In Russia, did Vallejo's and Mandelstam's paths cross? Not that he notes. But not impossible. Tsevtaeva? Akhmatova? Pasternak is among those he does. It remains to be seen whether our albatross will make the publication of those seven discrete volumes more or less likely.

Cited translations of Vallejo

Tungsten, trans. Robert Mezey (Syracuse, 1988), Mulligan uses his own translation for the excerpt in *Selected Writings*

The Black Heralds, trans. Barry Fogden (Allardyce, Barnett, 1995), the opportunity is taken here to amend "toy windmill" in "Fresco" to "pinwheel"

The Complete Poetry, trans. Clayton Eshleman (California, 2007), latest of the translator's various versions

Against Professional Secrets, trans. Joseph Mulligan (Roof, 2011), the different article "Against Professional Secrets" is not part of this work

The Complete Poems, trans. Michael Smith, & Valentine Gianuzzi (Shearsman, 2012), gathers together earlier Shearsman volumes

A Poet's Fate

I'd like to write about J. H. Prynne and George Oppen. I
have. I've written about J. H., in the guise of Jeremy, for his 80th birthday
festschrift. Probably I need to leave it at that. I've reviewed a book, in retro-
spect overgenerously, about George for a journal. Neither are Antonyms
though bits of them have that character. I don't find it easy writing about
contemporaries, near contemporaries, those I have known. Every now and
then I might manage a word or two. I am not a reviewer. I know what I like,
sometimes, and what I do not like. Sometimes I think I know what to do.
Hence Agneau 2. Hence *Snow lit rev.*

✳

Here are some moderated bits from that review. If they appear impression-
istic, a trait I am quick to criticize in others, it is because I do not know
quite where to tread. "Think how careful George has been" I wrote in
"A Note About George Oppen", later allusively retitled "Note Through
a Lens", in which I related the reading, and the writing, of a poem with
walking and wandering in the mountains. Of course, care is not enough.
Without risk there is no meaningful, useful, process and progress.

Where is the poet's fate? Where is such a fate to be found except through
the process and, after a point, the absence of progress? I think that in a
wildly different way Oppen sought for poetry the same as Ezra Pound—as
did, for example, Laura Riding, for that matter: profound ethics, which
were they not, and where they are not, mistaken for moralities might hold
true. You see, too much is expected of poetry, don't you think? In Pound's
case that was his way to fragmentary excess. In Oppen's to fragmentary
effacement. But do I err? Oppen noted "There are situations which cannot
honorably be met by art, and surely no one need fiddle precisely at the
moment that the house next door is burning", which suggests that poetry's

limitations did not deceive Oppen. No, I do not err. If Oppen had not expected too much of poetry he may not have needed to articulate such a proposition because there would be no opportunity to be, or at least to feel, let down—which is not to say that this explains Oppen's oft-cited twenty-five year silence in the writing of poetry. Far less important than commentators would have us believe.

I think—I am often thinking—Oppen was a philosopher without philosophy. That doesn't matter because a poet's philosophy will never amount to much more than a partial attempt to justify or explain that particular poetry. Only the poem can be held to account as exemplary or rotten, or somewhere in-between, not its sources, those that are objective—the language, shall we say, which appears as a ready-made above one's head, at the ready to be remade—and those that are subjective—I shall say only, if evasively, that we know all about that. So, not about Oppen but about the implications of being Oppen.

For Oppen, born into wealth but not exactly happiness, his life's work included not only writing poetry and an early publishing imprint but engagement with communism, in practical liberal working ways rather than Party bureaucratism, and honourable World War II service. His readings of such as Hegel, Heidegger, Maritain were fruitfully naïve. He was ambivalent about his Jewishness, and about the Marxist thinking that influenced and, after the war, necessitated his and Mary's decisions. About the silence he noted: "Don't know if I was right. But I was right not to write bad poetry —poetry tied to a moral or a political (same thing) judgment". How reminiscent of Akutagawa Ryūnosuke, who in "Hero" "tried his hand at writing a poem of tendency", in which piteous irony reflected his earlier marginalia "What a comedy" in his copy of I. D. Levine's *The Man Lenin* (1924). For the Oppens, literary and artistic aspirations were kept very much away from Party affairs. Yet engaged disaffection with communism was to take a lot longer for the Oppens than for the quickly astute Akutagawa and even longer from the point of view of the MacCarthyism that hounded the Oppens into exile in Mexico.

Somewhere among his essays Osip Mandelstam discusses what for him was the social meaning implicit in punctuation. For Mandelstam, punctuation expressed the conversational, the willingness of the writer to address, and to be addressed by, the reader. For Oppen, punctuation came more often to be defined as the poem's lineage and spacing. He wrote: "I would like the poem to be transparent, inaudible" and "I am forced to express myself in the simplest language I can find precisely because I do not use a colloquial language: there is no social tone which I am able to accept". It is possible to say, then, that both Mandelstam and Oppen were silenced by their poetry. Might some 1977 words by Andrea Zanzotto have been spoken almost as well by Oppen? "The world of poetry is one of mistakes, hallucinations, torpors, windings around nothing, in which one rarely stumbles upon the golden bough." Walking, wandering, winding, stumbling.

Oppen's private papers: jottings, drafts, reworkings, ruminations, many assembled into what have come to be known as "Daybooks", not a word Oppen gave them himself, have begun to surface. At first, extracts appeared piecemeal in reviews and a critical study. It is indicative of the breadth of the papers that not one item transcribed in that study is to be found in *George Oppen: Selected Prose, Daybooks, and Papers*, ed. Stephen Cope (California, 2007). This book is a real problem. I once went so far as to describe it as reprehensible. It should be no poet's fate to be represented by a volume of such selections from a huge corpus never intended for publication, at least, not in any knowable form, in which deepest thought to most foolish utterance is laid bare outside any real context. It is all right, excellent even, to draw upon such materials in the course of analysis but not to part-publish as a dedicated volume. How choose? Add to that numerous errors in transcription presentation—and I mean errors, not debatable interpretations —as revealed by the reproduction of sample facsimile pages and you have an unreliable mess. It is hard to explain away. Transcribe by all means but what is needed is a fascimile of the whole, however unwieldy that may be, or nothing. As for the poet's fate, it cannot so easily be determined.

*

J. H. Prynne's poems are not usually so transparent. Yet: "Probably no writ-er of our time, except possibly Ezra Pound, has had a higher conception of the writer's calling, his obligations to his art and to his reader." Clarence Brown wrote that about Osip Mandelstam. Let us apply that equally to Prynne. And let us apply that equally to Paul Celan and Andrea Zanzotto. Etymologists, philologists, ethicalists, all. Yes, "to his art and to his reader." I refuse to be intimidated by so-called difficulty or those critiques on diffi-culty, positive or negative, that have infected our academic and popular literary cultures both. I shall not include Prynne's own "Resistance and Difficulty" in that because his essay is a model of clarity. Prynne's poems belong to the reader, scholar or otherwise.

Prynne is a terribly important poet, and essayist—where is the long procrastinated collection of his critical prose? An absolute necessity as was putting out the original edition of his *Poems*. From the opening "The whole thing it is, the difficult" to the closing "you say stuff it." Much more has followed. The poet's fate? For the moment, I must leave it there. But here let's get rid of the appellation experiment, for good.

NOTE

Anthony Barnett, "And You Too", in *For the Future*, ed. I. Brinton (Shearsman, 2016), 80th birthday festschrift for Jeremy Prynne

—, review of P. Nicholls, *George Oppen and the Fate of Modernism* (OUP, 2007), in The *Use of English*, vol. 60, no. 2 (Spring 2009), error about Edmond Jabès–Oppen–AB not noted

—, "A Note About George Oppen", in *George Oppen: Man and Poet: Paideuma*, vol. X, no. 1, (Spring 1981); revised as "Note Through a Lens", in A. Barnett, *Carp and Rubato* (Invisible Books, 1995), repr. in A. Barnett, *Poems &* (Allardyce Book ABP, 2012)

Osip Mandelstam, *The Complete Critical Prose*, ed. J. G. Harris (Ardis, 1979)

Akutagawa Ryūnosuke, "Hero" in *A Fool's Life*, trans. A. Barnett and Toraiwa N. (Allar-dyce Book, 2007), rev. repr. in A. Barnett, *Translations* (Allardyce Book ABP, 2012)

Andrea Zanzotto, "Self-portrait", in *The Selected Poetry and Prose of Andrea Zanzotto*, trans. P. Barron (Chicago, 2007)

Clarence Brown, *Osip Mandelstam* (CUP, 1978)

Right to Left

Early writing systems, many of them, were written either left to right or right to left. Later things settled down one or the other in different parts of the world. I do wonder why I have a tendency to open a book or leaf through a magazine in the Chinese or Japanese or Hebrew or Arabic direction. Right handed. Holding it in the right hand and leafing with the left. I wondered whether this was a common phenomenon so I conducted a little survey. Not uncommon. Not so common. A vestige of the past.

Nervous Apprehension

Nervous apprehension in preparing to write. Does this make sense? I should draw what is holding me back because I cannot visualize the line.

COLOURFUL TIGER ROCK wants me to keep her mail. She doesn't want it forwarded. She doesn't want it opened. I can't say this is a good idea. Burying her head in the sand. Can't be bothered. No one knows what might or might not be important. Probably nothing is, of course. I remember my mistakes. And flowers.

✻

COLDS take four days to come four days to stay and four days to go away.

✻

white a project What is this ridiculous word *project*? Why is white a project? He could do with an editor.

✻

NON-CREATIVE ROTTING to call these writing classes by their true name.

✻

COLOURFUL TIGER ROCK is a dancer, a maker, a thinker, a dancing girl, who dances her way from one dance to another through Europe and beyond. From East to West to Middle. If I were looking for a story to narrate I would not have to look very far because she is in front of me. She is not tall and although her belly is flat with running and exercising she is wont to ask if she is getting fat. Ridiculous. Her face is that classical oval. Whether she lets her hair down or does it up in different ways it doesn't matter. As if nothing she can do to herself can unbeautify herself.

Proposal for the Reception and
Non-Reception of the Poet

UMBERTO SABA wrote *History and Chronicle of The Songbook* under a pseudonym. It "was not intended to fool anyone. It was a purely 'diplomatic formality.' Everyone knew that the author of the study on Saba's poetry was Saba himself." It is rather like that here. Except that this is not a study of a poetry, much as the poet would like to write it (unlike Saba, probably he does not have the patience or wish to revisit too deeply his biography, which might summon up what he would best like forgotten). Instead it follows one thread, which also runs through *History and Chronicle*: the reception and non-reception of a poetry infinitely attractive and fascinating, incomplete in its flaws. The flaws being both despite and because, or the other way round. Nor should it draw comparisons with other poetry contemporary with it. Comparisons will not work. Its attractiveness and fascination is true to itself and indeed one of its benign commentators—there are some—writes of the author he "is like no other poet of his generation, yet both his elliptical lyrics and his work in longer spans should be part of the current consensus of what constitutes our modern poetry."

Should he begin to recount the offences committed and the injuries done by mean uncomprehending spirits—he has on more than one occasion been one himself—which has usually been through silence, when ill words in public more than privately would have done better, there would be no end to it. Oh, that's as old as history so I am abandoning this proposal here and now to talk about Umberto Saba of Trieste.

*

I have eight volumes of translations of Saba in front of me. A ninth, a posthumous unfinished novella of adolescent sexuality entitled *Ernesto*, sits on the shelf outside the scope of this piece. Of the eight, one is the complete *History and Chronicle*, one is *The Stories and Recollections*, drawn from over 1500 pages of prose, two are selections of poetry and prose, the latest beautiful, the other virtually unobtainable having all but disappeared, and four are selections from the poetry alone, drawn from Saba's more than six hundred poems in the *Canzoniere* over 1200 pages.

Until 1978, Saba was represented in English only in anthologies. Very different from the attention given his colleagues Montale and Ungaretti. Joseph Cary's 1969 *Three Modern Italian Poets* is a substantial critical overview of these three poets, including interspersed poem quotes with literals. Robin Fulton's tiny 1966 *An Italian Quartet,* added the lesser Quasimodo. More than twenty years passed following Saba's death in 1957 before the first dedicated volume of his poetry appeared: Felix Stefanile's beautifully Verona-printed limited edition small selection from Elizabeth Press, reissued by a trade publisher in 1980. Stefanile's florid note, "Translating Saba", offers a rationale for his idiosyncratic approach and lists some occasional translators, including Thomas Bergin but also, evidently in error because there is no trace, Charles Tomlinson. Robert Harrison's 1986 *Umberto Saba: An Anthology of His Poetry and Criticism* consists of extracts from *History and Chronicle* and poems discussed therein. It might be said hardly to have existed from the moment it first came out. A mere handful of copies are to be found in libraries, one of which has come my way in photocopy. A trawl of used booksellers brings up nothing. Perhaps it was quickly pulped. Indeed, Harrison's versions of the poems are nothing to write home about but it did break new ground with lengthy extracts from the *History.* Ironically, the International publishing imprint suggests wide distribution. Well, one of those few copies is located in a library in China. It is probably no accident that Saba's novella of adolescent awakening, *Ernesto,* came out, in 1987, before any widely available comprehensive offering of his poetry.

In 1993, the year Cary's book was reissued in a revised edition, and his versions of "Trieste Poems" were included in his delightful memoir *A Ghost in Trieste,* Sheep Meadow Press embarked on a most welcomed long overdue publishing programme (which had the effect of reversing the fortunes of Saba and Ungaretti insofar as it brought a fair amount of Saba's prose into English, while Ungaretti's, though not Montale's, remained, and still does, largely unknown, such as a lecture and essays on Leopardi). At first with Estelle Gilson's translation *The Stories and Recollections*, including "The Jews", "Shortcuts", "Very Short Stories", "Recollections of the Wondrous World". Brilliant, informative, affectionate, wry. We would have liked more. Then, in 1998, with two volumes translated by Stephen Sartarelli: a worthy 300 page bilingual selection from the *Songbook*, and the complete *History and Chronicle*, in which Saba scrutinizes his work in a unique third-person critique. In between, Christopher Millis's small, a bit eccentrically translated, selection *The Dark of the Sun* appeared from a different press in 1994.

I do not often sing the praises of single volume selected anthologies that mix genres but I am glad to say Vincent Moleta's 2004 closely annotated 650 page *Poetry and Prose* from Æolian Press is a magnificent exception. Yet, despite 3 February 2006 acclaim in mutable *TLS*, in a review by John Taylor, which also considered Sartarelli's work, Moleta's volume is, rather like Harrison's fugitive mixed genre anthology, scarce, though not quite as scarce. Unlike Harrison's there are a good number of copies in libraries, though none with dealers and past website links are inactive. Nevertheless, it is available from the address given in the bibliographic note below. *Poetry and Prose* is a beautiful, chronological, contextually interwoven, presentation of Saba's poems with the originals, stories, commentaries including radio talks, and correspondence. Interspersed are some twenty-five colour images, mostly paintings of Trieste, related in one way or another to the poems, such as those by his friend Vittorio Bolaffio, Leonor Fini's portrait of another Triestine, his friend Italo Svevo, and a couple of manuscript reproductions. Moleta's fascinating subject-matter and metrical analysis is no dry dissection but, as he says: "it will help if it helps. Saba is, as he said, a coherent poet, in the sense that everything he wrote is interconnected. Nothing can take the place of careful reading". I believe Moleta's are the most believable of translations, alive to music as well as to method and meaning. Expensive it may be, given its weight, posted from Australia, but if one twenty-first century translation is to be read this labour of love is the one.

Why is it difficult for me to recommend as wholeheartedly the some 570 pages of George Hochfield and Leonard Nathan's bilingual *Songbook: The Selected Poems*, the latest, 2008, and most widely distributed translation? The jacket flap proclaims: "Until now, however, English-language readers have had access to only a few examples of this poet's work." Dishonesty or ignorance on the part of Yale–Margellos, perhaps, but even so. Its partial bibliographic citations seem to begrudge earlier translators. It reeks of excessive institutional funding. More to the point the translations read like translations. Pretty much at random, here is the first stanza of "In riva al mare", which also introduces, hardly accidentally, unless stupidly, a graceless innuendo in the last two lines, which the remaining two stanzas show, indeed confirm, to be absolutely unwarranted:

BY THE SEA

It was six in the afternoon, one bright
holiday. Behind the lighthouse, in that
place where one blissfully hears the sound
of a cowbell, was the voice of a boy
playing in peace among the wrecks
of old boats, sitting alone, close to
the open sea; I came, if I'm not mistaken,
at a climax of my human misery.

And here is Moleta's version—neither Stefanile nor Sartarelli translate this poem:

BY THE SEA SHORE

It was six in the late afternoon, a bright
holiday. Behind the Lighthouse,
where you hear blissfully the sound
of a bell, the voice of a boy
playing contentedly around the carcasses
of old boats, I was sitting alone
by the wide open sea; there, unless I'm mistaken,
I reached a peak of my human sorrow.

To my ears this is a wonderful English stanza. I don't even feel the need to give the Italian original. A couple more lines. Hochfield–Nathan: "Among the stones that I gathered to throw / into the waves (a floating beam / was the target)". Moleta: "Among the stones I was picking up to throw / into the water (a bobbing spar / was the target)". Not much difference? Woodenness versus fluency.

Saba of Trieste, terrified that the Austro-Hungarian city into which he was born might be taken from the Italy with which he so thoroughly identified; non-practicising Jew, on his mother's side, vehemently opposed to Zionism, buried in the Jewish section of Trieste's cemetery, "a stone's throw from Svevo"; proprietor of Libreria Antica et Moderna, now Libreria Antiquaria Umberto Saba, still located at Via San Nicolò 30^B; great poet of autobiographic—how inadequate the word is in his case—loves and vicissitudes, of small and great things.

For a moment I thought to finish with all the versions of Saba's "La Capra", and to let "The Goat" be the judge. But no, the last word need only be Moleta's:

> I spoke to a goat.
> It was alone in the field, tethered.
> Swollen with grass, sodden
> with rain, it was bleating.
>
> That monotonous bleating was kin
> to my sorrow. So I replied, first
> in jest, then because sorrow is eternal,
> has but one voice that never alters.
> I heard this voice
> groaning in a solitary goat.
>
> In a goat with a Semitic profile
> I could hear the plaint of every other grief,
> of every other life.

NOTE

I make no excuses for introducing a star system. Five should be tops but Vincent Moleta deserves six.

An Italian Quartet: Versions after Saba, Ungaretti, Montale, Quasimodo, trans. Robin Fulton (London Magazine Ed., Alan Ross, 1966), thirteen after Saba, bilingual

Joseph Cary, *Three Modern Italian Poets: Saba, Ungaretti, Montale* (New York, 1969; rev., augmented 2nd ed., Chicago UP, 1993), critical overview, poem quotes with useful literals

Thirty-one Poems, trans. Felix Stefanile (New Rochelle, NY, Elizabeth, 1978; Manchester, Carcanet, 1980), in fact thirty-one and a half, of which the half only is bilingual   * * *

Umberto Saba: An Anthology of His Poetry and Criticism, trans. Robert Harrison (Troy, MI, International Book Publ., 1986), unprepossessing trans. of selected poems   * *

Ernesto, trans. Mark Thompson (Manchester & New York, Carcanet, 1987; London, Paladin, 1989), unfinished adolescent rite of passage from homosexuality to heterosexuality novella, written 1953, deprecated by the author, posthumously publ. 1975, filmed 1979

"Nine Trieste Poems from the *Canzoniere*", trans. Joseph Cary, in Cary, *A Ghost in Trieste* (Chicago, 1993), in fact twelve, memoir, literary history, illus., bilingual poetry

The Stories and Recollections of Umberto Saba, trans. Estelle Gilson (Riverdale-on-Hudson, Sheep Meadow, 1993), selected prose   * * * * *

The Dark of the Sun, trans. Christopher Millis (Lanham, MD & London, Univ. Press of America, 1994), forty-three poems, uneven trans., bilingual   * *

Songbook: Selected Poems from the Canzoniere of Umberto Saba, trans. Stephen Sartarelli (Riverdale-on-Hudson, Sheep Meadow, 1998), thoughtful trans., bilingual   * * * *

History and Chronicle of the Songbook, trans. Stephen Sartarelli (Riverdale-on-Hudson, Sheep Meadow, 1998), complete   * * * * *

Poetry and Prose, trans. Vincent Moleta (Bridgetown, Western Australia, Æolian, 2004), bilingual poetry   * * * * * *   *Æolian Press, P. O. Box 606, Bridgetown, Western Australia 6255*
vincentbartolomoleta@gmail.com

Songbook: The Selected Poems of Umberto Saba, trans. George Hochfield and Leonard Nathan (New Haven & London, Yale–Margellos, 2008), awkward trans., bilingual   * * *

Bohumil Hrabal's Fascination

It has happened again. "What are you reading?" "Bohumil Hrabal. This one just out." "*Rambling On* . . . I don't know who he is. Quite an unpronounceable name." "I think you know him. He wrote *Close Watch on the Trains*, which was made into a film." "Oh, *Closely Observed Trains*. I remember that. A very good film." "Yes, there are two different translations" —afterthought, at least two.

I have already spoken about Hrabal. No one funnier. Even drunken tragedy around the inns of Kersko woods brighten the mood. "I convert the vale of tears into laughter". "I'm an anti-genius, a poacher in the game enclosures of language". In *Rambling On: An Apprentice's Guide to the Gift of the Gab Short Stories*—now, should there or should there not be a comma after *Gab* (Prague, Charles University, Karolinum, 2014), translator David Short notes his correction to *Fascination* of Hrabal's calling a recording by virtuoso pops violinist Helmut Zacharias *The Fascination*. "Where Hrabal got the definite article from is a mystery". Hrabal does play fast and loose with English names, often getting them wrong. This one is a sure case for correction, not least because the first of this famous melody's multiple appearances has it read right off the record label. Well, I'm not so sure. I mean, Short is right. The tune is indeed "Fascination" and the label says so. Funnily enough you can hear the Zacharias on the web. But I think it quite on the cards that Hrabal hasn't made a mistake. From his point of view it is *His Fascination* and therefore *The*.

There are numerous novels and not-so-novels by Hrabal available in English, with more to come. You just have to take your pick, all of them. But be warned. They could persuade even the most hardened teetotaller to head straight for the nearest pub.

True Musicians

A STATELY PHOTO OF JOHN TCHICAI, "calm member of the avant-garde", so described by Dan Morgenstern in his accompanying profile, adorned the front cover of the February 10, 1966 issue of *Down Beat*. I sought out the two 1965 LPS by the New York Art Quartet, which Tchicai formed with trombonist Roswell Rudd—their first eponymous—I hate that word— ESP-Disc, including a recitation by then LeRoi Jones, Amiri Baraka to be, and their second, *Mohawk* on Fontana. I was mesmerized. I was half-way through putting together *Nothing Doing in London One*, a letterpress review, loose leaves in a folder, of writing and the arts. I wrote to Tchicai in care of *Down Beat* asking him to contribute a score. Tchicai sent his composition "Quintus T" from *Mohawk*. Portuguese artist António Sena, living in London at the time, contributed to the same issue, which is how Sena came to make a drawing imaginatively based on Tchicai's three-page score. It was to become the cover of my book-length *Poem About Music* (1974). On 1st October 1968 I produced a concert by Tchicai's Cadentia Nova Danica at Wigmore Hall, where I recited my poem *A marriage*. It was the first jazz genre concert to grace that hallowed hall. On 2nd March 1969 I produced the *Natural Music* concert in Cambridge, with the unfortunate, notorious, participation of Lemono, names I can hardly bring myself to mention. I went on to play percussion with Tchicai in Denmark, occasionally in Norway and England, including 16th April 1977 at the Cambridge Poetry Festival with the Roy Ashbury–Anthony Barnett percussion duo, formed at the University of Essex. Ashbury's playing was more cerebral than my less schooled approach. Derek Bailey, Tristan Honsinger and Maarten van Regteren Altena were on the same bill. We all jammed together at the end.

NYAQ's drummer Milford Graves was my study bible for what was done, what could be done, with percussion. Tchicai wrote in the *Mohawk* liner: "Graves was present at our first rehearsal and played with us for about half an hour, and I must confess that this was a very pleasant surprise and more than that, because Graves simply baffled both Rudd and I in that we, at that time, hadn't heard anybody of the younger musicians in New York that had the same sense of rhythmic cohesion in poly-rhythmics or the same sense of intensity and musicality." I would go further. I swear Graves is capable of playing two notes, the second fractionally before the first. Big Sid Catlett could do that too. Yes, work that one out. I tried to learn too to lift notes up into the air, not to beat them down into the ground.

One day a cassette arrived out of the blue. A July 17, 1981 Soundscape, New York duet by Tchicai and Graves, during which Tchicai recites my poem "Drops", from *Blood Flow*, in call and response with the audience. Tchicai left us in 2012, a few months after I met up with him at a recital in Brighton where suddenly he opened a book and once again deconstructed a poem, though which one I cannot recall. Tchicai himself wrote better poems than many musicians. One appears in the noble-intent but, what can I say, politely, uneven *Silent Solos: Improvisers Speak*, ed. Renata da Rin (Köln, Buddy's Knife, 2010). Tchicai dedicated a copy "To my friend of many years Anthony Barnett, an improviser just like me", which reminded me of Johnny Mbizo Dyani's more than kind words when I blew out the contents tray of a match box to scatter, splatter like rain, forty- or fifty-odd matches over a drum head "You are a true musican". I wish I had the evidence that it happened but the tapes were disappeared. Yes, those are the words, they were disappeared. More about true musicians later.

In January 2009 my good friend and colleague publisher Torleiv Grue wrote from Oslo: "Did I tell you that I had a lunch with Amiri Baraka when he visited the Oslo Poetry Festival? As a gift I gave him your book *Listening for Henry Crowder*. He immediately started reading. He said the book was great. He was still keeping up with black music history. And this book was just the thing for him. You know." Wonderful. I am so glad he knew my book. I was not best pleased when my suggestion that I participate in the University of Kent's 2014 Baraka conference at the ICA in London was not taken up. Baraka passed on a few months before he was to be honoured.

Preamble out of the way—why shouldn't I set the record straight—I can turn briefly to what really prompted this piece. Triple Point Records have released *Call It Art*, a five-vinyl-album set plus coffee table sized book housed in a gated white birch box of all the previously unreleased recordings by the NYAQ in New York in 1964 and 1965 that have come to light. Rehearsals, recitals, broadcasts, a *Mohawk* outtake. Four hours of mostly beautiful music by Rudd, Tchicai, Lewis Worrell and Reggie Workman and other bassists, Graves, a few others, recitations by Jones/Baraka.

The accompanying book has informative chapters by co-producer Ben Young about the musicians and the recordings, guitar maestro and Rudd's friend Duck Baker musing on youthful discovery of the quartet's recordings, an itinerary, photographs, programs, ads, letters, ephemera. Most of this is to be welcomed but, it has to be said, there are moments when the extravagance of the documentation takes on the appearance of a triumph of design over content. One example, close to home, has the title page and, inexplicably, and on a different page, one and a half only of the three published pages of the score of "Quintus T", reproduced from *Nothing Doing in London One* without citation.

Clearly, or not so clearly, I have dabbled in a kind of poetry and jazz —*Composed Poetry and Improvised Music*, a tour with writer Douglas Oliver and *The Diagram Poems*, trumpet player William Embling and saxophonist Evan Parker; performances of *Poem About Music*, one with Tchicai, one with Bailey [see also"Beckett and Jazzality"]. Really I do not think these things work particularly well. *Poem About Music* is precisely about how it is, perhaps?, only possible to music about music, which hypothesis is perceptively worked through by Joseph Persad in his dissertation on the poem—see endnote. In *Listening for Henry Crowder* I go a little way towards recounting the dubious evolution of jazz and poetry, as opposed to song settings, citing Charles Mingus's "Freedom" at *Town Hall Concert* as a rare success. So I have to be ambivalent about the recitations with music by Jones/Baraka.*

In the post-Ornette Coleman–Don Cherry era, a number of musicians have had the most profound impact on my musical thinking and appreciation. Among them, to name only a very few, trumpet player Wadada Leo Smith, violinist Leroy Jenkins, The Revolutionary Ensemble with Jenkins, violinist India Cooke, cellist Abdul Wadud. Smith articulated what should have been obvious all along. Sounds are determined by the silences that come before and that follow. To put it the other way. Silences are determined by the sounds that come before and that follow. First and foremost I was mesmerized by the New York Art Quartet. Fifty years on I still am.

Rudd wrote in a 1964 notebook *"intentional* incoherence sometimes a cop out / Due to the morality of music, the *responsibility* of the (improvising performer) composer is in direct proportion to the degree of his *intuition.* The intuition is sometimes muddied by lack of excecution, unless the incoherence is intentional. Whatever his bent, to master the art of incoherence or blatant clarity, he should be precise (or precisely *imprecise*). To be imprecisely imprecise one need only be a beginner." This is why I have always been a beginner, musically speaking. I look back in wonder and gratitude at the opportunities I was given to work with true musicians, who were not beginners, if indeed they ever were.

NOTE

New York Art Quartet (ESP-Disc, 1965), mono, reissued on CD

New York Art Quartet: Mohawk (Fontana, 1965), mono, stereo, stereo reissued on CD

New York Art Quartet, 1964–1965: Call It Art (Triple Point, 2012), mostly mono, four hours of previously unreleased recordings on five vinyl albums with book

I discover that for fifty years I have been listening to the mono release of *Mohawk*, now rectified with the purchase of a copy of the stereo LP release reissued in Japan in the 1980s

Performances by other versions of the NYAQ are too different: two albums from an autumn 1965 European tour with Finn von Eyben, Louis Moholo in place of Workman, Graves who could not make the trip; a 1999 *35th Renunion* (DIW), incl. Baraka, on which Tchicai plays tenor, the instrument he long before switched to from his alto of the original quartet; a 2002 Willisau, Switzerland video posted on the web with wrong-headed altoist John Zorn replacing Tchicai because of a contretemps, later patched up

John Tchicai, "Quintus T", in *Nothing Doing in London One*, ed. A. Barnett (London, 1974)

Anthony Barnett, *Poem About Music* (Providence, RI, Burning Deck, 1974), repr., incl. António Sena's drawing, in *Poems &* (Lewes, E. Suss., Tears in the Fence, in assoc. Allardyce Book ABP, 2012), the setting on individual pages in the original edition is preferred

D. S. Marriott, "Interview with Anthony Barnett", in *The Poetry of Anthony Barnett*, ed. M. Grant (Lewes, E. Suss., Allardyce Book, in assoc. Grille, 1993)

Anthony Barnett, *Listening for Henry Crowder: A Monograph on His Almost Lost Music* (Lewes, E. Suss., Allardyce Book, 2007), with CD, updated at www.abar.net/crowder.htm and see also "Henry Crowder's Letters to Nancy Cunard" in the present volume

Joseph Persad, "'you have spoken to me badly': Composition and Improvisation in the Work of Anthony Barnett" (Univ. Cambridge, 2014), MPhil dissertation

There are a few released recordings on which I play percussion, including *Afrodisiaca* by John Tchicai and Cadentia Nova Danica (MPS), recorded in Copenhagen in 1969 on the day of the moon landing, and *Upright at the End of Lippestad (Both Ways)* by improvising chamber quartet Muskap, at the Henie Onstad kunstsenter, Oslofjord, in 1975 (Prisma) but at the time of writing I am happiest with how I am heard, indeed how we are heard, on William Embling, trumpet and other instruments, and Anthony Barnett, percussion and other instruments, *The Lion in The Grove* (AB Fable XXABCD-2CDXXABCD1/2, 2015), recorded at the Bristol Arts Centre, 20th March 1980, in the presence of Wadada Leo Smith, with whom three years earlier I gave a recital at the University of Essex. This 2CD set is available from ABP. Among other recordings, I hope at least one of two sessions by Tchicai with the Roy Ashbury–Anthony Barnett percussion duo may find release

*Pondering these things is not new: "Every art should and must have its limitations, so they don't swallow each other up." "How to paint is something that can only be painted, not said." At the same time "Great art resides in great goings-astray,"—Robert Walser, "A Painter" (1902), in *Looking at Pictures*, trans. Susan Bernofsky (New York, Christine Burgin / New Directions, 2015)

The Procatinator

About the Epigraphs

The two epigraphs first appeared in *Antonyms & Others* without explanation. It might look as if the second is meant to be a translation of the first but it is not although there is certainly a connection from my point of view

The first epigraph is taken from Laozi, 5th–6th c. BCE. It has been translated in various ways but the one I like best is found in master of the antinomy Qian Zhongshu, *Limited Views: Essays on Ideas and Letters*, trans. Ronald Egan (Cambridge, Mass., Harvard University Asia Center, 1998), where it reads: "Right words look like contradictions"

The second epigraph is my own. There is ink in Asia that comes in blocks the colour of gold. But when one writes with it it comes out black

About the Procatinator

My grateful thanks to Naoko Toraiwa for visiting Anzumura, Apricot Village, and finding out that the artist who designed their wonderful sign of the cat is Jun Morioka, courtesy Anzumura, Hino-Shi, Tokyo